Appreciative
Leaders

In the Eye
of the Beholder

Edited by

Marjorie Schiller • Bea Mah Holland • Deanna Riley

The Taos Institute

Second Printing 2002

Printed in the United States of America.
ISBN 0-9712312-0-6

In all cases, the editors and writers have made efforts to ensure that text credits are given to the appropriate people and organizations. If any infringement has been made, The Taos Institute will be glad, upon receiving notification <www.taosinstitute.org>, to make appropriate acknowledgment in future editions of this book.

Thank You

We thank all of the authors who submitted manuscripts and those who said they would do so for a second edition of the book. We extend special thanks to Ken Gergen and Jane Seiling of the Taos Institute--to Ken for his appreciative leadership and to Jane for holding our hands each step of the process. We thank Dave Cooperrider who has been a consistent friend and teacher, Karen Barone continuity editor extraordinaire, and our technical friends Terry Heminger, Christine Major Theran, Gabe Fenigsohn, and Celia and Bob Morris. Thanks also to our colleagues Jim Ludema, Ada Jo Mann, Jane Perkins, Anne Radford, the staff at Pegasus Communications, and especially Arlene Beauchemin for being willing and more than able resources. We are also grateful for the support of our friends at Cape Cod Institute, and members of Appreciative Inquiry Consulting. Finally, thanks to our friends and families who have put up with us in an appreciative way!

A special thanks to the following authors and *leaders* who have contributed to the Appreciative Leadership Project:

Todd Brooks Irving, Texas	*Thomas White, Retired Senior Executive Vice President-Market Operations, GTE Corporation*
Mary Eaggers and Stas' Kazmierski Ann Arbor, Michigan	*Jan McNally, President, Covenant HomeCare and Senior Vice President of Covenant Health*
Tom Griffin, Algonquin, Illinois	*Jim Gustafson, Vice President and General Manager, MECHdata, Inc.*
JoAnn Javons Culver City, California	*Evelyn Turrell, Manager, Automobile Club of Southern California*

Ferne Kuhn Devon, Pennsylvania	*Andrea Gilbert, Senior Vice President Operations, Main Line Hospital, Bryn Mawr Campus*
Loretta Randolph Alexandria, Virginia	*Annette Sturdevant, President and CEO, Organization Development Systems, Inc.*
Rusty Renick Charlottesville, Virginia	*Pedro Cervantes, Vice President-Human Resources, Legal Affairs, and Public Relations, Avon Mexico*
Cheryl Richardson Aurora, Illinois	*Don Thompson, President, Midwest Division, McDonald's Corporation*
Jane Seiling Lima, Ohio	*Kenneth Gergen, Mustin Professor of Psychology at Swarthmore College and Director-Taos Institute*
Barbara Sloan Purcellville, Virginia	*Claudette Simpson, Director-Human Resources, American Chemical Society*
Ali Tocker Wellington, New Zealand	*George Hickton, CEO Tourism, New Zealand*
Jane Watkins and Ralph Kelly Williamsburg, Virginia	*Renata Price, Assistant Deputy Chief of Staff, Army Material Command*
Susan Wilkes Richmond, Virginia	*Dr. Grace Harris, Distinguished Professor, Virginia Commonwealth University*

Contents

Preface vii

Foreword ix

1. The Road to Appreciative Leadership 1

2. Taking Care of Business 7
   - *Lee Olivier, CNO, Millstone Nuclear Power Station, Northeast Nuclear Energy, Berlin, Connecticut*
   - *Ken Lang, Vice President, Upstream Technology Group, BP p.l.c., Houston, Texas*
   - *Bob Stiller, President and CEO, Green Mountain Coffee Roasters, Waterbury, Vermont*
   - *Margaret Crawford, Director-Human Resources, Harley-Davidson Motor Company, Milwaukee, Wisconsin*
   - *Michael J.P. Burns, Vice President - Human Resources and Richard M. Pellett, General Manager, Hunter Douglas Window Fashions Division. Broomfield, Colorado*
   - *Ricky Lewis, Manager-Real Estate Operations, South/Virginia, Verizon Communications, Durham, North Carolina*

3. Supporting Wellness 63
   - *Michael B. Green, President and CEO, Concord Hospital and Capital Region Health Care, Concord, New Hampshire*
   - *Thomas S. Inui, M.D., President and CEO, Fetzer Institute, Kalamazoo, Michigan*
   - *Dr. Sarah Eagger, Consultant, BKCW Mental Health NHS Trust, London, England*

4. Serving the Community 97
   - *Chief of Police Peter L. Carnes, Yarmouth Police Department, Yarmouth, Massachusetts*
   - *Kathleen A. Mullin, Director of the School-to-Career Programs, Boston Public Schools, Boston, Massachusetts*
   - *Annette T. Griffin, Superintendent, Carrollton-Farmers Branch School District, Dallas, Texas*

5. Reflections of a Lifetime 127

- *Dr. James A. Norton, Emeritus President, Central Washington University, Ellensburg, Washington*
- *Dr. Bernard Lafayette, Director-Center for Nonviolence, University of Rhode Island, Kingston, Rhode Island*
- *Dr. Warren Bennis, Distinguished Professor of Business Administration, University of Southern California, Los Angeles, California*

6. The Method, the Model, and Making Meaning 157

Appendix 169

- *Interview Protocol*
- *Interviewer Survey*
- *Interviewer Biographies*
- *Related Resources*

Preface

Kenneth J. Gergen

I take great pleasure in introducing the work of Marge Schiller, Bea Mah Holland, Deanna Riley, and their colleagues as the flagship volume in the Taos Institute Focus Book series. The Taos Institute is a non-profit community of scholars and practitioners working to explore and extend the view that through human relationships we construct our realities. Our attempt is to design and promote creative, appreciative, and relational practices for broad use within society and around the world. Through publications, conferences, workshops, and educational programs, we hope to provide innovative conceptions and effective practices for transforming individuals and organizations.

The Focus Book series is intended to bring to a broad readership significant fruits of these efforts. The particular hope is to make available cutting edge ideas and practices as they are developing, and at an affordable cost. Our champagne glasses are now raised at the publication of *Appreciative Leaders: In the Eye of the Beholder*!

This present exploration of Appreciative Leadership is indeed cutting-edge work. The enthusiasm with which organizational practitioners have greeted Appreciative Inquiry is both exciting and gratifying. Practices of Appreciative Inquiry are now employed around the world, in organizations of every variety. However, practitioners are also increasingly aware that such practices harbor implications of far greater depth. The transformational processes set in motion by appreciative inquiry are not limited to these particular practices alone. The powerful processes of appreciation may thrive in all domains of organizational life. The domain of leadership is an optimal venue for unleashing these forces.

It is in this context that we owe a great debt of gratitude to Marge Schiller, Bea Mah Holland, and Deanna Riley. They have not only witnessed these powers at work, but have now taken the first significant steps in bringing them to light so that all may share. Their method is a simple one: To work with their colleagues to identify leaders who seem to embody practices of Appreciative Leadership, and explore with them what it is they do and how they understand their actions. The results are far from simple: Here we have an enormously rich body of material—a broad array of insights and ideas coupled with diverse forms of relevant practice. As they are shared with us, the readers, we are challenged to rethink the character of organizational life and are provided images to inspire our own future actions.

These resources come to us at a crucial time in the history of organizational life. In many sectors, the traditional organization— hierarchical, top down, and rigidly structured—is proving unserviceable. The demands of an increasingly complex and rapidly shifting environment bring about new demands for flexibility, coordination, and the sharing of opinion. Further, with increased sensitivity to the ways in which organizational viability depends on the values and voices of many different groups, concerns with the democratization of the workplace have become paramount. These changes call for new practices of leadership. In my view, it is just such practices that are represented in the pages of this book. We encounter here the contours of the future.

Kenneth Gergen
Director
The Taos Institute
July 2001

Foreword

David L. Cooperrider

In the decade since our book *Appreciative Management and Leadership* was written (Srivastva and Cooperrider, 1991), I have become increasingly convinced that *appreciative modes of management may be to our newer, self-organizing systems what deficit or problem-oriented methods of management have been to command-and-control bureaucracy.*

Appreciative Leaders: Theoretical Background

Deficiency focus, root cause analysis, remedial action planning, closing gaps, intervening in broken down systems, machine metaphors—these were and still are among the most recognizable vocabularies of bureaucracy, and these are the vocabularies, when caricatured, that make us all shudder and laugh when reading one of the all time best selling management books, *Dilbert's Management Principles*. Robert Haas, chairman and CEO of Levi Strauss, observes that the deficit management approaches have reached the point of diminishing returns, and that the kind of radical innovation needed today requires whole new patterns: "'There's a whole range of behaviors that were highly functional in the old hierarchical organization that are dead wrong in the flatter, more responsive, empowered organization that we're seeking to become'" (Haas, in Bennis, 1992, p. xi).

At the core of every distinctive form of social organization, proposes Barbara Marx Hubbard (1999), are "memetic codes" that are to social systems what genetic codes are to biological organisms—"the way genes build bodies, memes build cultures, societies, and the noosphere." So when Thomas Kilman (1979), for example, equated deficit-based, problem-focused management as the memetic essence of what it means to be an executive, he was likely speaking about the modernist, bureaucratic form of industrial organization. He wrote: "One might even define the essence of management as problem defining and problem solving, whether the problems are well-structured, ill-structured, technical, human, or environmental" (p. 214).

But this book describes something completely different. It's about a new memetic code. It is about leadership as a life-centric process of reality construction and meaning-making, *not* leadership as machine repair. It is about the "spirit of inquiry" being even more powerful in leadership than final answers and intervention, and it is about the amazing energy that is available when we realize that organizations are centers of human relatedness, first and foremost, and relationships thrive where there is an appreciative eye and when people see the best in one another, when they share their dreams and ultimate concerns in affirming ways, and when they are connected in full voice to create not just new worlds but better worlds.

Appreciative Leadership in Practice

Appreciative Leaders: In the Eye of the Beholder, describes and tells *stories of positive revolutionaries*, of leaders who are transforming their industries and the world through appreciative modalities of knowing, interrelating, and the active social construction of reality. It tells the story of leaders who lead by valuing, not evaluating, and who create change by synthesizing or combining capacities (not breaking apart the problematic) and by imagining the new, the better, the possible in ways that compel, transcend, and uplift. Peter Drucker was perhaps the clearest and closest to what this volume is about when we asked him the question last summer: What will the core of leadership be in *tomorrow's* organizations? His reply was immediate and unequivocal: "The task of leadership is *to create an alignment of strengths and make people's weaknesses irrelevant.*"

Over the last couple of years, I have been having remarkable conversations with leaders who represent this emerging paradigm: President Jimmy Carter; Jim Staley, President of Roadway Express (featured in *Fast Company*); Dr. Bernard Lown, Founder of the Nobel Prize winning organization, International Physicians for

Prevention of Nuclear War; Anita Roddick, Founder of The Body Shop; Tom White, former GTE officer; Admiral Clark, Chief Naval Officer, Navy; Jane Pratt, CEO of the Mountain Institute and former officer at the World Bank; and Dee Hock, Founder and CEO Emeritus of Visa. What all of these human beings have in common, as far as I can discern, is an uncanny capacity to see, magnify, and connect all that is good and best in people and the world around them, and to summon all that is best in life as something that can only be described as a "power core" capable of mobilizing transformational conversation and cooperative action. Several themes appear again and again:

- *Everything the appreciative leader does conveys to others a genuine, respect-filled, positive intention to produce enduring change for world benefit. Reality, for the appreciative leader, is not a given: It is there for our active shaping in the direction of our higher purposes.* For example, when I asked Jimmy Carter to describe for me moments in his work when he feels most alive, effective, and fulfilled, he said: " I know precisely the moment. It is when we have put the last nail in the structure for a new Habitat for Humanity home...the whole group stands together in front of the home in a circle, and we say a prayer, celebrate, and talk. We are together as equals, Black and White, across all racial boundaries and all class boundaries—and you see right in front of you the tangible image of our joint capacity to deal with poverty. At those moments, you feel miracles of benefit to people are possible...and the tears often well up in my eyes." Today Habitat for Humanity is making more homes than any other corporate or nonprofit homebuilder in the world.
- *The appreciative leader enlarges everyone's knowledge and vision of the appreciable world—all the strengths, capacities, and potentials—not by having solid answers, but expansive questions. It is precisely through inquiry itself that the appreciative leader realizes and unleashes,*

not their own, but other people's genius. The art of leadership lies in the art of the positive question. One of the most exciting pieces of work I have ever done was a three year project with Dee Hock, the Founder and former CEO of Visa. When I asked Dee about the Visa story—it went up 10,000% in profits under his leadership—he pointed to the moment he brought a brilliant team of "ordinary bankers" together to re-conceive, not just the old Bank Americard, but the very concept of organization itself. In his memoirs, Dee Hock (2000) writes: "I asked if they would be willing to take a week or more of their time, isolate themselves completely, <u>set aside all thought of the problems of the system</u>, and address a single question based on a simple assumption: *If anything imaginable were possible, if there were no constraints whatever, what would be the nature of an ideal organization to create the world's premier system for the exchange of value?* After a bit of head shaking and rolled eyes, they became intrigued..." (p. 132). The Visa system, soon thereafter to be born, became a benchmark of a new "chaordic" form of organization—and within a decade it had become the largest corporation in human history. The appreciative leadership lesson? *We live in worlds our questions create and, precisely because of this,* humility is a stronger quality of leadership than bravado, infectious curiosity more important than supervision, and a spirit of inquiry is more decisive than static strategy.

• *The appreciative leader lives with an awareness that organizations that are in "full voice" will be more creative, resilient, and knowledgeable than organizations that are in half voice and, because they hold positive assumptions about people, they, as leader-weavers, are continuously expanding the web of inclusion—realizing that the best in human beings comes out when people experience the wholeness of their system.* Jane Pratt, the CEO of the Mountain Institute and former officer at the

World Bank, taught all of us about this when she helped create a worldwide alliance of scientists, grass roots activists, UN Agencies, and non-profit environmental groups to deal with the environmental threats to mountains in all parts of the world. The web of inclusion she helped create was hailed in 1997 by the UN. What she set in motion was a worldwide movement that would make people as aware of our fragile mountain regions as we are of our precious tropical rainforests (Kaczmarski and Cooperrider, 1999). Rodrigo Loures, taking inspiration directly from Jane, said, "It is not just systems thinking we need; what we really need is *living* systems thinking—to put it into practice." So what did he do? He closed down his whole Brazilian food plant and brought all 750 people of Nutrimental Foods together for four days, to plan the future of the company. It was an extraordinary display of trust, but it paid off. A year later absenteeism rates were cut by 300 percent and profits were up 200 percent.

Similarly, Jim Staley, President of Roadway and just featured by *Fast Company* magazine (Hammonds, July 2001, p. 56), did the same thing. He brought truck drivers, dock workers, union leaders, customers, and people from every function of the company together to plan the future. His belief in dialogue, in relationships, and the human factor is total. "There is not a lot of technology that's going to make us more efficient. So future opportunities are going to come from our people being engaged and involved in the business, and coming together as a whole helps us align, create, and empower in ways we have never experienced before."

I was at that four-day meeting. And Jim Staley worked in a subgroup just like everyone else. He only stood up once, on the morning of the last day, and spoke spontaneously for seven minutes. After he spoke people cheered and gave him a standing ovation. He lifted up, in inspiring and grateful words, what was in the heart of every person at Roadway. People sometimes talk about participative management as abdication of leadership. But this kind of radical participation—bringing a whole plant together—is not abdication, but just the opposite. Leadership is given life by relationship, by good conversation. The more relationship, the more leadership. This is what the web of inclusion is about.

These are the kinds of insights Marge Schiller, Bea Mah Holland, and Deanna Riley have brought together in this wonderful book. Listen to what they and their partners have to say. Appreciative leaders are maestros. They brilliantly work with relational capacities, strengths, invisible opportunities, values, elevated qualities, assets, generative words, patterns and currents of possibility, meaning systems, sacred traditions, stories that inspire—almost anything but machine-like breakdowns. Appreciative leaders bring the gift of new eyes, penetrating and positive. They hone in on capacities. They lift every voice. But most of all they are agents of knowing life—generating alternatives, lifting up options for better living, and creating webs of inclusion that serve to enlarge our world-making potential at its healthiest. There is a world where you are, where we are. It exists because of what we, collectively now and socially before us, have constructed. And it is made up of so much potential just waiting to be used to create, like a painter does before going to a canvas with paints of red, and blue, and yellow.

May this daring book open new options in your leadership. And may it help all of us expand our constructive capacity, our life-centric capacity, for bringing our *appreciable worlds* into closer and closer alignment with our language, our accounts, and our conversations of our *appreciated worlds*. For in the end, appreciation is as much a language as it is a quality of relational living—it is, as Bill Moyers once put it, "a language of life."

David L. Cooperrider
Weatherhead School of Management
Case Western Reserve University
Cleveland, Ohio
July 2001

Chapter One

The Road to Appreciative Leadership

Marjorie Schiller

Something is happening with leaders. They are changing. As our views of how organizations' work changes, the models of effective leadership also change. Gone is the notion that organizations are like machines: You plug them in, you turn them on, you replace broken parts, and productivity results. There is an emerging picture of how organizations *actually* work. As we move from the mechanistic metaphor to a more subtle and complex understanding of organizations, we see the need for leaders who care about context, wholeness, and interconnectivity. We are moving from solving problems to embracing the iterative mystery of solutions. We have learned that what we ask determines what we find and what we appreciate matters. It appears that information and interrelationship are the building blocks of new organizations and the motivators for the appreciative leaders who are the topic of this book.

The Elements of Appreciation

Appreciation has three core elements. First, as the dictionary suggests, an act of appreciation acknowledges what is outstanding or special. Second, appreciation recognizes the mundane or ordinary. This suggests appreciation of the expected; taking joy in the unexceptional like the sky, a child's continual questions, and the day-to-day beauty of life. Third, there is appreciation of those situations that are painful and difficult; appreciation of the improbable and important lessons that are embedded in some of life's awful experiences. The Webster's Collegiate Dictionary offers "value," "prize" and "esteem" as synonyms for appreciate. Appreciative is also defined as "capable of showing appreciation." A leader is "a person who leads others along the way, a guide." Appreciation can also be defined in financial terms as in to appreciate or grow in value. You will see these definitions brought to life in this book.

1

The Purpose of the Book

This book was written for appreciative leaders to recognize their own style and to bring to the attention of learners and practitioners a more articulate and transparent model of appreciative leading. The demographics of the new work force suggest more people will have more choices about where to work and how to work. Job satisfaction and appreciation are vital to attract and retain the highest quality employees in the new economy. Therefore, leadership skills and attributes must shift from giving orders to providing direction and support.

Appreciative Leadership, as indicated in the following chapters, is highly values based. Leaders see it and recognize it as their own personal style of leading—"that's just what I do." Yet, Appreciative Leadership is more than an individual style. It is a method and practice that is gaining respect in the international business community. This book aims both to connect appreciative leaders, so they may know and recognize each other, and to encourage new leaders to see the benefits of bringing Appreciative Leadership into their workplace practice. The book also attempts to codify what was originally seen as stylistic or idiosyncratic and to reinforce and give language to models of success in appreciative leading. We want to demonstrate that Appreciative Leadership works. The appreciative leader is one who is as Miracle Grow® plant food is to a garden; that leader can jump start growth and, when it really works, can produce change at the speed of collective imagination.

Two Assumptions

There are two underlying assumptions to this book: 1. Everyone is a leader. We all lead in different domains; therefore, everyone can learn from this book. 2. Leadership is in the "eye of the beholder." The relational (what happens between people) co-construction (mutual development) of meaning (interpretation) is the foundation of what we experience as real.

This book has been written as an invitation to leaders to recognize themselves in the stories of others. Appreciative leaders want theory and examples that validate and communicate what they are already doing. This book is also written for people who are in the process of finding their own leadership style. We want emerging leaders to see some applicable alternatives to command and control methods. As organizations become more like self-organizing systems, and as the rate of change increases, we propose that there is a benefit to celebrating the existence of appreciative leaders as examples of doing leadership better and doing leadership right.

Methodology

One hundred and ten people were approached and invited to interview and write about an appreciative leader. We intentionally did not provide a definition, but used the "you know one when you see one" approach. More than half of those invited identified a leader they wanted to interview. Then more than half of those who expressed interest submitted a manuscript. What you will read in the next five chapters is a selection from the submissions. The interview demographics are explained in Chapter Six; it is noteworthy that 43% of the submitted interviews were with women appreciative leaders, and 11% were with international appreciative leaders from Europe, New Zealand and Latin America. To get the big picture and expand your knowledge of appreciative leaders, read more interviews at the Taos Institute Web site <www.taosinstitute.org> or the November 2001 edition of the Appreciative Inquiry newsletter <www.aradford.co.uk>.

The leaders who are profiled are varied and diverse. The aim is to show Appreciative Leadership in action. This is not an academic book, although it is expected it will be useful to teachers and students. It is a series of snapshots, sketches, and drawings of leaders whose behaviors and philosophies of leadership are congruent with the principles and practices of appreciative inquiry.

The authors have provided insight into how these leaders make meaning of their jobs and lives. Efforts have been made to give the reader descriptions of what the leaders actually do in order to make Appreciative Leadership tangible and visible. The choice to use first names, last names, titles, and combinations in describing these leaders was deliberate. The nuances and language of personal or relationship titles is a complex business. Words create worlds,

3

and it is important to show the diversity and changing nature of relationships.

- Chapter Two describes the Appreciative Leadership stories and experiences of seven leaders who are taking care of business in profitable companies.
- Chapter Three brings together leaders in the health care field who focus on medical service delivery, wholeness, and healing.
- Chapter Four highlights the experiences of several community leaders and their contributions in police work and school systems.
- Chapter Five shares the reflections of three people, each with a lifetime of honorable leadership.
- Chapter Six presents the editors' findings and insights along with an Appreciative Leadership model derived from the interviews that were conducted.

The title of the book, *Appreciative Leaders: In the Eye of the Beholder*, underscores our individualized definitions of "appreciative." This is why interviewers were asked to select appreciative leaders based on their own perceptions and knowledge of Appreciative Inquiry—a concept of finding the best in organizations and promoting positive change through inquiry into the finest of what was, what is, and what might be. Conversational exchanges and relationships clearly define the qualities of appreciation. Appreciative Leadership can look very different in different settings: an appreciative leader in the U.S. Department of the Army may sound different than the appreciative leader in direct sales or telecommunications.

While the title of the book deals with the potential multiple interpretations of an individual's story ("what is appreciative to me, might not be appreciative to you"), it is through the reading of many stories that one can begin to piece together the overarching characteristics that define an appreciative leader. The editors could have approached this book as market researchers and held focus groups with leaders, or as academic researchers and surveyed the

4

catalogue of leadership literature to find the salient qualitative data. Instead, a more anthropological approach—going in search of leadership ethnographies—was selected. Each author—or would-be anthropologist—was supplied with identical question protocols. Assuming what is asked predetermines what is found, we asked appreciative questions. What we heard were stories and answers that reflected the appreciative leadership of successful women and men. The authors expanded the protocol questions with their own follow-up and/or augmenting inquiry. This protocol is included in the Appendix. Each author questioned, listened to, and observed their leader and, much like Margaret Mead or Jane Goodall, documented the individual nuances of style and culture. It is in the intersection of these personal accounts that we found the universal. In the last chapter the editors describe the fourteen characteristics that identify, personify, reinforce, and drive appreciative leaders. We identify the themes that emerged from our study and present a model of Appreciative Leadership.

We want future and emerging leaders to see the pragmatism and the promise of Appreciative Leadership. Leaders, and those who study and work with them, have been having a lot of conversation about moving beyond command and control to a new style of leadership that we believe is called for in organizational life now and in the future. The hope is that readers will see Appreciative Leadership as the template for leadership in this century.

Conclusion

We invite you to read and learn from these stories of successful women and men who enable others to expand their own definitions and design their own philosophy of leadership. These leaders are not confined to any industry or culture. The stories can remind us of the leaders we want to be and give us *aspirational* clues of how much further we can grow. Here are practical strategies to appreciate, and models to use as we travel the road to being appreciative leaders.

We have learned a great deal and we hope you will too.

Chapter Two

Taking Care of Business

This chapter presents the stories of people who lead in a wide range of businesses. In this series of sketches, Lee Olivier turns around Millstone Nuclear Power Plant, Kenny Lang navigates the startup of Upstream Technology Group within British Petroleum, Bob Stiller dreams and builds Green Mountain Coffee Roasters, Margaret Crawford leverages the Human Resources capabilities within Harley-Davidson, Ricky Lewis adds value as a mid-level manager at Verizon, and Richard Pellett and Michael Burns live a co-leadership model within Hunter Douglas. Throughout all of these examples, the leaders demonstrate how their personal beliefs materialize in their noteworthy organizations and beyond.

Best of the Best
Leon (Lee) Olivier, Senior Vice President and Chief Nuclear Officer, Millstone Nuclear Power Station, Northeast Nuclear Energy, Berlin, Connecticut

Judy Otto

Leon (Lee) Olivier is now senior vice president with Entergy Nuclear Northeast, in charge of merging two co-located nuclear plants formerly owned by separate companies. Lee was senior vice president/chief nuclear officer of Millstone/Northeast Nuclear Energy, a subsidiary of Northeast Utilities, from October 1998 to March 2001, after 29 years at Boston Edison.

When Lee Olivier showed up on his first day at Millstone Nuclear Power Station in November 1998, he took on a nearly impossible challenge. As the new Chief Nuclear Officer, the highest level manager on site, his daunting task was to turn around what he termed a "reactive, legalistic, patriarchal system…[infused] with mistrust horizontally and vertically, [and establish] an atmosphere of fundamental trust that would enable safe and profitable operations."

Millstone, a one-time giant in the nuclear power industry, located on Long Island Sound in Connecticut, had three reactors capable of pumping out 2700 megawatts of power per hour and, in a deregulated market, would have produced roughly $2,500,000 in revenue per day. However, the plant had been shut down in 1996 by the Nuclear Regulatory Commission (NRC) because of unsatisfactory regulatory performance. Nobody wanted another Three Mile Island or Chernobyl.

In 1998 Millstone had close to 2000 employees and 900 contract workers on site, as well as several managers on loan from two other nuclear power companies. Olivier's four predecessors had all quit or been fired, all within four years. Millstone was losing $1,000,000 a day. Employee complaints were so numerous and so serious that an Employee Concerns Program had been formed to monitor what was called the Safety Conscious Work Environment. What made Lee think that he, having briefly headed up another nuclear plant in Massachusetts, a plant one-third the size of Millstone, could succeed here? Lee was not the typical power plant executive.

As executive coach to Olivier's direct reports, the vice presidents/officers, I got to witness Lee Olivier's extraordinary capacity to overcome obstacles that had defeated his four predecessors. With fascination I watched this 50-year-old—up through-the-ranks product of a large Irish and French working-class family—consciously and skillfully use an appreciative approach to create an organization no one had imagined possible. The turn around was not just about profits; it was about morale, respect for diversity, and empowerment. This was about optimism and positive thinking. But most of all, this was about a sense of purpose—Lee Olivier's purpose.

"I came to set a different table," Olivier told me, "to move from a top-down traditional hierarchy to a collaborative, inclusive organization." His key was to tap into the "unlimited human potential of the work force, ...to help them be aware of opportunities, ...to consciously and frequently set new horizons." He did this without the usual tactic of clearing the decks of current high-level managers. Olivier took his vice-presidents, directors, managers, supervisors, and employees on an adventure none of them could ever have imagined.

"Paint the picture for them," Lee always advised his managers as they set goals for their people. The picture of the Millstone recovery was an artist-commissioned picture, painted in bold colors: a ship sailing through and around various nautical impediments in order to reach the goal, being back on line, once more generating power and revenue. A representative group came together and worked with the artist to portray the voyage they were determined to take. They suggested sharks in the water, rocky shoals, and pirates to represent the barriers. A clear, sun-drenched horizon represented the goal. Did any of them really believe it possible after all they had been through? Olivier made sure they did believe.

One of his first site-wide initiatives was to bring the Pacific Institute's, "Investment in Excellence," training on site for all the employees, and later for their spouses and children. The program is based on cognitive science and teaches people how to reach desired goals through positive self-talk. People compose affirmations about a desired future state, and draft the affirmation as if it were already true. Applications to personal and family life are encouraged.

Fortified by new, positive thinking and a clear vision of the future, Millstone employees were engaged in another training program that put people through "Boot Camp" to learn Continuous Process Improvement. Boot Camp graduates then redesigned business processes, reorganized work groups, and reassigned job responsibilities. Once more, it was the employees, having been given tools, authority, and confidence, who began to make sweeping changes that would bring Millstone back to full power and themselves back to a sense of contribution and pride.

Lee himself adhered to the advice given to leaders: communicate, communicate, communicate. He was a presence in the plant, often donning protective clothing as was required by anyone entering the Radiological Controlled Area. He held frequent "All Hands" meetings in the employee cafeteria. He held "10% meetings," where each department sent 10 per cent of its work force to hear and take back to their co-workers Olivier's challenging and inspiring messages. Lee held "In Touch" sessions with employees where he listened and responded to spontaneous questions, concerns, and suggestions. He began these sessions with the questions, "What's on your mind?" or "How are you feeling?"

I witnessed Lee achieve an extraordinary outcome to a potentially volatile meeting. An employee, beset by work and personal problems, had murdered his wife and then committed suicide. The employee's co-workers were understandably upset and, finding no rational explanation to this horrible event, were determined to place the blame at Olivier's feet. Olivier sat down with this group of about 15 people, and acknowledged their grief, as well as his own. Then he asked them how they were doing. They vented, they grieved, and they discovered they were doing so to a sympathetic listener. The more Lee listened, the closer they brought themselves to a more peaceful place. Then they asked Olivier to respond. When he finished sharing his thoughts and feelings, one of them spoke for the group: "We're behind you all the way, Lee."

In addition to listening, Olivier gave his people more pictures. He helped them see what was happening at Millstone. Progress charts, graphs, and documents started to show up on bulletin boards and on the intranet. A color-coded Key Performance Indicators system gave people a clear and colorful picture of current and desired performance. Olivier himself identified the critical "stakes in the ground." Once more he used a metaphor to convey a clear message. Each goal that was achieved raised morale. There was no stopping this plant now. They were on a critical path to success, a path toward the audacious goal Lee had set for them, to be the "Best of the Best."

Yes, there were glitches, none serious, but even a minor setback could cause the fragile morale to plummet. Lee made sure that didn't happen. He constantly encouraged his employees, reminding them of the goals and repeatedly expressing his appreciation and confidence in them. In addition, he always modeled the behavior he expected. I never saw him lose his temper or publicly reprimand or embarrass anyone. I'm told he had candid conversations with his direct reports, but it was always done in private.

I attended numerous meetings that Lee held. I always marveled at his capacity to build on others' ideas, to acknowledge points of view opposed to his own, and to maintain an atmosphere of trust, collaboration, and innovation. Early in his career at Millstone, he instituted two significant regularly scheduled meetings: the weekly Station Alignment Team (SAT) meeting and the monthly Officers' Retreat. SAT meetings were attended by the six officers, the 15 or so directors, and various other appropriate managers. Olivier's intent was to build a collaborative team that learned together, problem solved, and supported one another in their managerial responsibilities. Most of the meetings were strictly business. "The first SAT meetings," Olivier said, "were extraordinarily painful, until there were some wins." A few necessary meetings tackled the hairy issues of morale and interpersonal issues among the members of the group. They backed down from very little.

The monthly Officers' Retreat was a daylong meeting where tough issues were hammered out. As the officers' coach, I attended all but one of these retreats over nearly a two-year period. At the beginning, the officers were experts at undermining each other, perhaps more because they lacked an awareness of potential synergy than because of ill will. In one-on-one coaching sessions, I would learn how they planned to take on one another at upcoming meetings. Because of the coach's primary ethic of confidentiality, I worked indirectly to help them prevent competition and deal with differences in a productive way. But it was always Lee who set the tone for synergy and the clear expectation for collaboration. Otherwise, my coaching would have had no positive effect.

Most of the officers reporting to Lee were long-term Millstone employees who carried with them the legacy of a failed plant. They also brought management and interpersonal styles significantly different from Olivier's. For example, the pool for nuclear power employees came from the nuclear arm of the Navy, so managers from that background brought a militaristic, authoritarian style. Furthermore, most of these officers were engineers, skilled in analysis and interested in detail versus the big picture. They loved getting their hands dirty in the minutiae of, for instance, a leaking valve, and rarely ascended to the level of long-term strategy. Although they were highly competent and innovative in their technical areas, they were not at Lee's level of organizational strategy, or as interested in the people issues. The military value of loyalty to the leader, however, compelled them to stand behind Olivier's initiatives. In doing so, they learned how to be better leaders.

A trained optimist, Lee knew that if he could tap into the officers' potential, their loyalty would be replaced by skill. He spent time figuring out each officer and saw that "each one would bring something different to the table." "You want a balance," he said, and he was determined to figure out a way to optimize those differences and make the team work. He learned to interact with each one differently. For example, one worked best in very focused conversations; another liked to talk at length about issues, bringing in history and using many anecdotes. In all of his interactions Lee fostered a climate of inquiry rather than the authoritarian atmosphere he walked into on his first day on the job.

Walking into that organization was an act of pure optimism, which Olivier says he was born with, but was shaken out of him as a child. As a younger manager, he claims to have been more judgmental and critical and "learned that the people were different from what I expected. So I became more reflective, more appreciative." Lee believes that some people are born optimists but most of us need to study and focus on optimism. He has found Martin Seligman's book, *Learned Optimism*, helpful. And Lou Tice, founder of the Pacific Institute, has become Olivier's model for affirmative thinking and living. Olivier stated, "There is no other approach in life…you can attain more, achieve more. People will gravitate toward and follow optimistic leaders."

The ironic fact is that, in his early years, Olivier himself had little encouragement from others. His parents had their hands full with a large family and Lee was left to his own resources. He was not what one would call a model student, but one of his teachers, a nun, saw that spark in him. Much later in his life, a CEO at his former company had "an intuitive appreciation for what I could do, and he showed it in more than words." But the words made it clear. "You can go places…you can do it…you can get people to follow you," he told Lee. As Olivier put it, this executive "blew on the ember." More recently, Olivier found a mutually supportive relationship at his former company in a boss who was keen on innovation.

Olivier is not the type of person, however, to wait for mentoring and encouragement to show up. His spirit of inquiry and self-efficacy is obvious as he searches far and wide for answers, learning from experts he will never meet in person. Through his reading he consults with such diverse teachers as Wayne Dyer who wrote *How to Manifest Your Destiny*, Robert Spitzer, who wrote *The Spirit of Leadership*, Thich Nhat Hanh, author of *Living Buddha, Living Christ*, and Susan Jeffers, author of *Feel the Fear and Do It Anyway*.

In Olivier's Millstone position, encouragement during the most difficult challenges came from the CEO of Northeast Utilities, the company that owns Millstone. The company's Nuclear Committee of the Board of Directors has always backed Olivier, although they admit that at first they weren't sure how, or whether, he could actually succeed in the midst of so many barriers, and so much negative history. In the summer of 2000, the Board acknowledged Lee's leadership when Millstone received an "exemplary performance rating" from the Institute of Nuclear Power Operators, a self-regulating agency within the nuclear industry, whose standards are higher than those of the NRC. In their letter to Olivier, the Board said, "It is evident that Millstone Station is well on the way to achieving its goal of nuclear excellence."

At the same time, a local newspaper, "The Day," headlined Millstone success with "NRC Plucks the Monkey from Millstone's Back." The newspaper wrote:

Once an embarrassing example of how a nuclear station should not be operated, the Millstone Nuclear Power Station has come full circle and is now back in the good graces of its federal regulators...after years of intense regulatory scrutiny....By any measure, Millstone has come a long way from January 1996 when the NRC placed the station on a "watch list" of problem plants. For more than two years regulators would not allow any of the reactors to operate because the problems had become so pervasive as to endanger safety....A great deal of the credit for this achievement goes to Millstone's chief nuclear officer, Leon J. Olivier.

Olivier credits his success to his "internal compass," which helped him retain faith along the way. "You can get derailed if you're not patient while building the foundation," he said. How did Olivier acquire such an accurate internal compass? "From Eastern mysticism...being completely open and non-judgmental, which leads to possibilities...and awareness of opportunities...and a belief that human potential is unlimited."

Clearly, Lee Olivier is his own best example of realized potential.

Confidence And Conversation:
One Leader's Touchstones
Ken Lang, Vice President, Upstream Technology Group, British Petroleum p.l.c.
Houston, Texas

Bernard J. Mohr

Kenny Lang is a 20-year veteran of the gas and oil industry and currently VP of Upstream Technology, for BP. His group provides technical expertise to BP's 60 business units worldwide, as well as carrying out research and development. Kenny oversaw the integration of Upstream Technology during the merger between BP and Amoco, and later ARCO.

"There is not much in the world, there's not much in life, there's certainly not much in business that can't be dealt with by getting a few smart people around the table. And hence, the only thing missing is a conversation. It's only when conversations fail to occur that breakdowns happen."   Kenny Lang

At the end of our interview, Kenny leaned across the desk and asked, "May I tell you my feelings about this interview?" "Of course," I answered, not quite sure what he was about to tell me.

When we started this interview I'm sure you could sense my low energy and distraction. I had other things on my mind. In fact, I've really been struggling with some reorganizing we are doing and with a whole new set of responsibilities I've taken on. It's been an uphill process. During the course of answering your questions, I'm aware of how much better I feel, how much more confident in our collective capacity to move forward I feel, and how much more energized I am—thank you for this interview!

As I've come to learn, this is vintage Kenny Lang; unassuming, candid, and invariably appreciative. I first met Ken (he prefers Kenny) Lang when he opened a one-day inquiry into Passionate Leadership for his extended leadership team of about 70. I had arrived that day to co-lead the inquiry with Neil Samuels, British Petroleum (BP) Exploration's Manager of Learning and Organization Development. In response to a request for "training leaders to be more passionate," Neil had called me and asked if this would make an appropriate subject for an inquiry. "Sure," I said, "but the big question is, will Lang support something so different from more traditional training?" Not only did Kenny enthusiastically receive and support our proposal, but about one year later, largely because of his leadership and willingness to take risks, BP is using Appreciative Inquiry as an approach to partnerships, outsourcing implementation, performance management, management audits, innovation, and safety.

As a company, BP is achieving extraordinary results within its industry—and those results come from commitments to extraordinary goals by senior managers like Lang. In fact, when I heard about the goals he had committed to, I wondered what sort of opening comments he might make on the day of our first large group inquiry. Would he give a "burning platform" speech? Would he raise the specter of dismissal for those of his subordinates who did not perform? In retrospect I'm not surprised by—but still in admiration of—Kenny's actual delivery. Instead of describing the size of the obstacles to overcome, he talked about the capabilities of the group. Instead of focusing on the urgency of action for survival, he talked about the enormous opportunity these targets represented for the group to live into its fullest potential. And yes, on the issue of consequences he did not threaten or badger his employees. He simply said, "And if we don't meet these goals, chances are I won't be around for long, so I'm asking you to work with me and with each other as best you can." Almost a year to the day that I first met Lang, he agreed to this interview—at a time when he was, as they say, up to his butt in alligators, yet he still found time for the following interview. So sit in on the interview now and join me in finding out more about this emerging leader.

BJM: Peter Drucker, considered by many to be the father of modern management, recently said, "Leadership is about creating an alignment of strength and making people's weaknesses irrelevant." What have you learned in practical ways about bringing out the best in human beings in groups and organizations, and how do you go about doing that?

KL: That's an interesting quote. If taken literally, it can be at odds with a lot of traditional practices that focus on shoring up deficiencies. I'm sure he's still desirous of that, and he's probably right that if you focus on what people are very strong at and can do well, and place them in positions where they will succeed, they'll be successful. This creates confidence, and confidence gives people the strength to do things that they otherwise might not—to take some chances. Actually having that strength allows them to address some of their deficiencies as opposed to just throwing them into precarious circumstances.

I just had what people call appraisals or father/son chats, with one of my bosses. He had asked me about this new responsibility I had been given, when I said, "You know what's interesting? I feel like I've become a much bolder leader and I think it's because you've shown so much confidence in me. And that confidence that you've shown in me has given me confidence to do things I don't think I would otherwise do."

I realize now that Andrew was practicing a kind of appreciative management style that has been profound in my personal development. This has been a big revelation for me. Now I try to do the same thing with my reports. I try to show confidence in people by giving them increasingly bigger positions, bigger accountabilities, things that I know they can do. I speak with them about my confidence in their capabilities to do what they might be timid about. For example, in this latest reorganization the positions I'm creating are big. In offering a number of people these jobs, I noticed they were very twitchy about taking them—because they're concerned and anxious about, *"Can I do what you're asking me to do?"* I could have said, "Well, not to worry, we'll find something," but instead I said, "I wouldn't ask you if I didn't think that you were capable of doing that." Had I shown anything less than complete confidence, it would have created self-doubt.

BJM: Your story focuses on bringing out the best in the people by showing your confidence in them. Is this one of your touchstones as a leader?

KL: Yes. Of course this is sort of golden rule stuff, I think. People have shown me that what I think of them as their leader matters to them whether that's in an assignment given to them, a promotion, or simply asking their opinion about big issues. Just asking for their opinions signals "your opinion matters." I think everybody, particularly professionals, wants challenging work, the opportunity to influence big issues and big decisions, and to know that their opinion really matters—and it does matter to me.

BJM: Reflecting back over your own career, tell me a story about a time when you were appreciated by somebody—instances when you recall being shown that the person had much confidence in you and did appreciate you.

KL: I have two stories. The most recent of course is the increase in my accountability for Upstream Technology. I mean, it's something that I've wanted for a while and I think will make a big difference in terms of simplifying things for the organization—and it's something that shows my boss's confidence in me. But I have another story. In 1997, I was up in Alaska, accountable for all the development of Prudhoe Bay. I did not have a technology position at that time. Lo and behold, I got a phone call out of the blue from Andrew McKenzie who was head of technology for the group. He asked if I would become technology director for reservoir engineering and wells, which was at least a two-grade jump from where I was. Andrew and I didn't know each other all that well and I was not at all the traditional sort of technologist usually picked for these positions. But Andrew decided that he had a different model in mind and wanted me to do that job. And basically, at every turn he met with me, made sure that I had the right support, and always committed to my success.

BJM: How did he show those things—commitment to your success and getting you the support?

KL: One thing he did, which is unique to anyone I have worked for in my 20- something years, is once a quarter I found something in my diary, about an hour-and-a-half meeting with Andrew. Now this is a guy who is very, very senior in the company and once a quarter he made it his business to meet with me. He just showed up, and he showed up in my office. He didn't say, "Come to downtown London, and meet with me." He showed up in my office and said, "How's it going? I just wanted to let you know I think you're doing a great job. Here are two or three things you might want to think about. Are there any things that you need from me?" And he did that once a quarter for probably at least a year and a half, which I thought was an amazing commitment to someone's success. That did a lot to create confidence in my own self about what I'm capable of. Knowing that there is a person out there who was willing to help me break down some barriers and give me the support I need, and was there for help—well, I thought that was really powerful.

BJM: It seems like the value of that kind of connection, that kind of feedback, that kind of support has been as important as the other kinds of work resources that you have access to—money, etc. I wonder if you could just tell me a little bit more about your best experience in being able to create parallel kinds of experiences for the people that report to you.

KL: I've tried to make what Andrew gave me available to all of my reports in terms of creating time and certainly sending the invitation out for them to book time with me. I've said, 'Let's

19

just talk about what *you* want to talk about for an hour or so,' as often really as they need.

I'm thinking about the time of the merger when I was asked to combine former Amoco and former BP technology processes and organizations, into a single global group, which has become what we now call Upstream Technology Group (UTG). People from Amoco and BP who didn't know each other suddenly became part of a single, unified, leadership team. For the first year to eighteen months we legislated that we were going to meet monthly face-to-face for two days and just spend time together rolling up the shirt sleeves and working on issues. We weren't going to use email to do these things. We needed to actually be together. We had to create a relationship among these folks of genuine mutual respect for each other and for me, and me for them. The only way to do that is through face-to-face conversation.

Another thing was, although each individual clearly had a very sharp area of accountability, when we came together as a leadership team we took off those hats and we then were the leadership team for the whole. Everyone had to be willing to hear what the other people had to say about things that would be traditionally their line accountability. So we tried to create an atmosphere that made that not just okay, but expected. That environment, I think, helped to create a group of leaders who very much appreciate and desire feedback and input into areas that are traditionally their accountabilities.

The other story is about when we said we wanted to create some passion around our leadership. And not the "from-the-pulpit" sort of passion, but real excitement and real commitment in our 750 people across the world—letting them know that what they're working on really matters, and it's importance to the future of the company. Ultimately, it was about, "How do we create confidence in everybody in the organization, so that every member of the organization is very confident?" Part of that was actually going down this path of Appreciative Inquiry—getting people to a place where they can reflect on their 15 to 20 years of experience, and tell stories about some very, very powerful times and moments when things worked extremely well for them. Times when the leadership was doing what the leadership needed to do to help them be successful, and times when the environment was rich with the right nutrients for them to be successful. When people go back and conjure that up and think about it, it gives everyone a sense of power over the present circumstances, to re-establish that as a way of being in their day-to-day work environment. So we've actually spent a great deal of time and continue to invest time and energy in helping people get to that place. I mean, it's really no more complicated than getting people to see that the cup is half full.

BJM: In clearly successful mergers, people find a way to cooperate and collaborate after the merger. You may be familiar with the Hindu greeting of "Namaste" which is like "Hello" but with a larger definition. I believe it means, "May the God in you meet the God in me and together we are one." This is perhaps a "culturally different" way of saying that when two different companies, organizations, or divisions are merging, collaboration and cooperation seem to occur effectively when each sees, elicits, and works towards the best of what the other brings to the table. So...if you were to give some advice to people who are merging what would you tell them?

KL: When I was bringing together Upstream Technology, BP plus Amoco included about 1300 people distributed around the world. That was when oil was at $10 per barrel and of course we assumed that prices might stay at that level forever. So we sized ourselves and thought about ourselves in that regard—which was probably not a bad thing at the end of the day. But what it meant was we eventually had to reduce the numbers from 1300 to 700 and learn to work together quickly. Whenever we were together, I would remind us that no one had the market cornered on good ideas. Amoco had a tremendous heritage around technology, invention, and innovation. BP on the other hand, had a very strong heritage of cost control and performance management. What one had, the other one was weak at, and what the other one had the other was weak at. It gave us both—in an instant—an opportunity to rebalance and to redress areas of deficiency. We just said, 'Let us suspend, for a moment, what's right and what's wrong, and let's just explore strengths.'

BJM: Did you consciously use that language—talking about exploring strengths?

KL: Oh, absolutely! In fact, we consciously did not carry forward the language of BP or the language of Amoco. We very consciously said it's something new and we will invent new language to talk about this. We created a third language to use for the merged organization. My new management team was quite literally split 51/49. We tried to get 50/50 so that every group could see that they had not been taken over, that the good things that they had were preserved and brought forward. It wasn't BP dominated or Amoco dominated—it was sort of a merging of the equals, and a merging of strengths. It worked out great. It really has made a huge difference in the way technology is thought about in BP.

BJM: The role of language is critical and with your new creations you effectively painted new pictures of who the group was. With that as backdrop, I want to move into asking you your thoughts about the connection between positive images and positive actions. Aristotle once said, "A vivid imagination compels the whole body to obey it." He was, I think, suggesting that imagination is what comes first and your body moves in the direction of imagination. Einstein, several hundred years later, said, "Imagination is more important than knowledge." If these things are true, if the power of image in organizations is so critical, how do new, dynamic, and compelling images of the future get created? Where do they come from?

KL: Traditionally, of course, it's always been leadership's job to come up with the vision. In some respects you can't deny that's very important. A compelling vision put forward by the senior most leadership of where we want to take the corporation is very mobilizing. People want to be a part of that future that's being painted. And I think that that's good and right, though it's sort of insufficient. There are much smaller issues that we all face from time to time—such as coming up with a new well completion, you know, very nuts and boltsy things. Having people who can think very broadly and are open to the possibility of doing things very differently and being encouraged to do that, will inevitably lead to breakthrough type technologies, created by people who feel like they have this invitation to innovate. We have to paint the picture that everyone can innovate and we have to make people believe it's an imperative.

BJM: How do you communicate that invitation, the expectation to innovate?

KL: Well, we don't have the market cornered on this. I think it's something you're always striving to do in a big organization. However, communicating that we expect our people to be innovative can be done in a way that is de-motivating to people. For example, if we say "You are not innovative, would you please become innovative?" that's not the right question because it paints a picture of them as non-innovative.

Innovation, I think, comes in a number of ways. It comes by a challenge being set. In other words, "Necessity is the mother of innovation." That "necessit" comes through leadership establishing some very challenging goals, goals that we don't know how to achieve through traditional means. In that challenge a call for innovation is implicit. But then leadership needs to recognize that people need some space and some time to be innovative— and they have to support that.

BJM: What is the role of leadership in providing support?

KL: We actually set aside $6 million and created what we call an "Innovation Board" in UTG. We began by acknowledging that all of our people are grinding away from seven in the morning to seven at night. They're just busy. So we knew we had to create space and time. We said, 'Let's create a board that's predominantly comprised of people who have made their names as being highly innovative, people who really recognize innovation when they see it— not managers by and large. And let's give them a budget of $6 million. Let's tell the whole UTG organization that all good ideas will be heard. If you've got an idea that you believe could transform the business, no matter how wild, put it on a one-page piece of paper, describe it, and submit it to the board. Within a short space of time they will get back to you.' I said I wanted at least 600 ideas in a year's time and that we would probably fund 30 to 50 of them. I wanted at least two, big, what I call, "Aha's" to come out of it.

I knew this would be worth six million times a hundred because we are a very capital-intensive company. We spend about seven billion dollars a year in capital and probably that much again on operating costs. Very small changes to performance replicated many, many times over yield huge benefits. So this was a way to create space, to legislate some time for people. If someone submitted an idea and it was a good one, people would say, "Yes this looks like it could have real potential. Let's give them the three to four weeks and the $200,000 to go away, work this, and bring it back."

This has only been going on for about six months and we've had well over 200 ideas come through. It's just now getting up and running at a good pace. We've had one idea that we declared as a big "Aha." It is a way of very powerfully signaling to people that their ideas matter, that we want to hear about them, that there's a mechanism in place for them to bring these things forward and they don't have to fight and scrap to be heard.

BJM: For the last hundred years or so, somewhere around 99 per cent of research in psychology has focused on studying various forms of pathology, causes and cures for schizophrenia, causes and cures of depression, causes and cures of what makes people become serial killers, etc. For the first time in the history of the organization, the American Psychological Association is actually lobbying for and putting significant funds into studying healthy people and is trying to understand what creates healthy people. In that context, the question I have is, 'What's the importance and the significance of positive thinking in your life: as a human being, as a parent, as a leader?'

KL: I have been an optimist for most of my life and I think it's the only way to be. I took a course in the early 1990's called "Manager of the Future" that actually helped shape a lot of this thinking. It was not just managing *in* the future, it was about managing the future. It was about being superior over circumstances and not being a victim. In other words, being a victim or deciding to be superior to the circumstances is a choice. You don't have to be a vice president, a manager, or a team leader; it's about choosing to put issues subordinate to your capabilities. That to me is very much a relative of optimism. If you believe that you have the capabilities to control circumstances, or at least you always have the ability to control your reaction to circumstances, then that is hugely powerful. It doesn't mean you can solve every problem, but it says if I can't solve it, I know that I can go to someone who can help me solve it. It means I never need be a victim of what is going on so long as I'm active.

Another phrase they used is, "The only thing that is ever missing is a conversation." If you just dwell on that and think about it a little bit, you realize that if the things that come up in life can be dealt with through dialogue, you can overcome them. There is not much in the world, there's not much in life, there's certainly not much in business, that can't be dealt with by getting a few smart people around the table. And hence, the only thing missing is a conversation. It's only when conversations fail to occur that breakdowns happen.

Therefore, optimism is an imperative for good leadership. So much of the organization takes their cue from leaders. If they hear that you are optimistic about the outcome, whatever the issue is, that you have confidence in yourself and in the organization, then they will be positive. When people are positive about their abilities to achieve outcomes, well, I think that's infectious. On the other hand, cynicism is just as infectious as optimism. People often say, "It would be okay if only "they," whoever "they" are, would fix things, do things differently." We all get paid far too much money and have far too many accountabilities to be looking for "they." Nine times out of ten it's purely within our gifts to make things different in a very positive sense.

BJM: If you think back on your journey to becoming the kind of leader that you are now, starting when you were in high school and going through the years, are there two or three moments that stand out as critical experiences that have shifted the way you look at the world?

KL: I think that the two biggest things that have shaped my whole life—everything about me—are meeting my wife and becoming a Christian. I've been married practically since birth; I was married when I was twenty and she was actually a little bit younger than that. I look back in time and think it's a miracle that people stay together that long. In the 26 years we have been married my wife has been incredibly supportive. She put me through university and worked so very hard. Also, I am not a hugely religious person, but becoming a Christian was life-changing. Look at some of the Christian values and ideals around treating people right, treating people the way you want to be treated, and really understanding—taking the time to understand how people would like to be treated. Even if you aren't a religious person, isn't that the way you should live your life anyway? Even if you were sort of a "dyed in the wool" atheist, there are certain principles here that transcend religion. They're just sort of what I call "right". And I think that going through that transformation actually instilled very deeply in me some of those values. So those are probably the two most important events.

26

And then I've just always been a pretty tenacious person about setting my mind to things and sticking with it. I've been fortunate to work with some people who are very, very good. People, I believe, I can always learn from. In each position I've held in the company, I have gone out of my way to understand how they lead and do things, and to learn from them. A guy I worked for in Alaska had a phenomenal ability to focus. He really taught me what commitment was about. He used to say, "Failure plus a good excuse doesn't equal success." Also rather than just giving something a good try, when you've made the commitment you need to turn over every stone, and ask for help. Asking for help is actually a sign of strength, not a sign of weakness. If you've got people's commitment and support behind you, and you've taken the time to get alignment, then very few things can create enduring obstacles.

BJM: Thank you.

KL: That was good. I enjoyed that. You know why I enjoyed this? May I tell you my feelings about this interview….

Creating The Conditions For Success: Finding The Best In People And Challenging Them To Live It

Robert Stiller, Founder, President and CEO, Green Mountain Coffee Roasters, Waterbury, Vermont

Ilene Wasserman

Robert (Bob) Stiller is founder, president, and CEO of Green Mountain Coffee Roasters. He was the champion and sponsor of one of the early whole-system appreciative inquiries with business process teams in a for-profit setting. Since then, GMCR has continued to apply the principles of appreciative inquiry to performance improvement, team-building sessions, and strategy development.

In the small Vermont town of Waterbury, on a field scattered with picnic tables, Green Mountain Coffee Roasters (GMCR) set up a tent within and around which it celebrated its twentieth anniversary. The company's 500 employees converged on the field from offices, the manufacturing facility, regional operation centers, and sales offices up and down the East coast. Both the backdrop and the familiar way the employees interacted recalled the firm's inception in 1981. But the number of people working with the company and other pertinent figures such as sales and stock price, clearly showed that GMCR has grown and is growing remarkably.

Green Mountain aspires to be the nation's leading specialty coffee company by providing the highest-quality arabica coffees from around the world to customers in its targeted markets. *Business Week* magazine recently rated it one of the "Top 100 Fast-Growth Companies in the United States." *Forbes* named GMCR one of the "200 Best Small Companies in America."

In the five years between 1996 and 2000, GMCR saw a 24 percent average increase in annual sales: from $33 million in 1996 to $84 million in 2000. Earnings per share in that period grew an average of 35 percent a year: from $.21 to $.60. In 2000, GMCR sold 11 million pounds of its 60 varieties of coffee to 7,000 clients. In the past three years, its stock price has increased nearly tenfold. And to think...it all began with a vision Bob Stiller created while sipping a cup of coffee in a small Vermont café twenty years ago.

If you ask people who work at Green Mountain Coffee Roasters what they are most proud of, they are likely to say they are proud to work for a company that walks its talk. They are proud to have a leader who backs up his words of caring with actions. Bob Stiller is that special CEO and leader. His commitment to his company's social mission and to the people who work for and with him is deeply rooted in his personal values and spiritual beliefs. He is committed to fostering a workplace that celebrates teamwork and the personal development of each member of the team.

A man of clear vision, Stiller believes in giving support to employees and encouraging them to be passionate. "If you really get connected to your passion, you can generate a different level of energy. I like to create the opportunities for people to find their passion."

The Green Mountain Coffee Roasters Story

Speaking of the company's goal to provide the "ultimate coffee experience" for customers, Bob Stiller exudes passion of his own, the passion he felt when he purchased the company in 1981. He demonstrates that passion with a commitment to social responsibility in Vermont, in target markets, and in coffee-growing areas. "I firmly believe that doing the right thing for the environment, for coffee growers, and for local communities helps us do well as a company and also yields satisfactory results for all stakeholders," he says. "I believe in the value people place in being part of a company concerned with more than just making money." The company's core values are not just a placard on the wall. The Green Mountain story makes these words dance:
- *A PASSION FOR COFFEE*
- *CREATING CUSTOMERS FOR LIFE*
- *A DESTINATION WORKPLACE*

29

- *ETHICS*
- *SOCIAL RESPONSIBILITY*

While many companies are making commitments to social responsibility, Green Mountain has been living the model. GMCR has:

- Supported a cervical cancer screening project for women in the mountains of Mexico.
- Provided start-up funding that assisted approximately 100 small-scale farmers in organizing a certified organic coffee cooperative in Sumatra, Indonesia. The project now accounts for 17 percent of all fair-trade coffee imported into the United States.
- Funded Coffee Kids, which helps families and communities in coffee-growing regions of Latin America find alternative sources of income so that children don't have to quit school to help their families pick coffee beans.
- Classified its Rain Forest Nut as a fair-trade coffee, which guarantees growers $1.30 per pound, nearly 50 cents higher than they would otherwise receive from other roasters.
- Dedicated profits from that Rain Forest Nut to help support biodiversity in the world's rain forests.

Closer to home, GMCR has encouraged employees to support a variety of local charities. Many devote hours to build Habitat for Humanity homes. In 2000, a group of employees shaved their heads as a symbolic act to solicit donations for a summer camp for children with cancer. Another employee has a national reputation as a volunteer for an organization that rescues golden retrievers. The company doesn't just support employees by allowing time off for service; it also contributes to and donates coffee for their fund-raising events.

Stiller talks about creating a "destination workplace": an environment that fosters teamwork, personal growth, and a healthy work-life balance. And he makes it happen. Employees take full advantage of educational opportunities, support for their community involvement, participation in self-improvement programs such as

Weight Watchers, and physical activities such as bike riding during lunch hours.

Knowing that their employer is devoted to giving back doesn't merely make employees feel good; it helps the company achieve productivity and retention. A 17-year employee in Operations says, "Bob truly believes we are working for a higher cause, and he inspires that in all of us."

Leadership Philosophy

Bob Stiller is committed to a culture that helps employees contribute to the best of their abilities—and beyond. "Leadership is about aligning strengths and making weaknesses irrelevant." People know the culture as one that seeks to find the right fit for employees. The company is replete with stories about people who were not working out in particular positions and were moved into other areas where they became valuable contributors.

One woman in Operations, for example, was having trouble getting along with other members of her team and completing her tasks effectively. Rather than fire her, Bob moved her to a position in Compensation and Benefits. She has since become a star contributor and is working on a special project to form an Employee Stock Ownership Plan. Was Stiller certain she would succeed? "No," he says, "but I had a hunch and followed it."

Others in the company share similar stories. A manager in sales, who moved an employee to a different position instead of firing him, explained: "That's not how we do it here. We first try to give people a chance in another position. You have to explore what they can do to contribute."

A Defining Moment

Stiller's leadership journey has been marked by incidents that were painful at the time but have since become significant sources of insight. More than a decade ago, three or four top leaders of the company were clearly interfering with Stiller's leadership. One person he trusted had taken over a role similar to that of chief operating officer. The man was threatening employees and blocking communication between Stiller and his staff members. It was a challenging time. Everything about who Bob was, and who he wanted to be, involved being trusting and supportive. Yet the man wasn't respecting that. Bob had to face the situation and ask the man to leave.

The experience has had enduring effects. "I'll be more careful about doing what's important to me and what I believe to be right." And it has reminded him of how important it is to have his own relationships with people.

Appreciative Feedback

When I asked Bob about the role he has played in fostering authentic relationships, sharing issues, and providing feedback, he spoke of the value he places on sharing his excitement in his team's and organization's success. "Growth happens when there is ability and skill that is invited to thrive. There needs to be a foundation of appreciation for people to thrive."

To achieve that, GMCR has taken an Appreciative Inquiry approach: Every employee has made some contribution. When they have contributed, what have they done? What can we learn from that? How could their success—small though it may have been—translate into more opportunity to express themselves in another function?

Appreciative Inquiry resonates with Bob Stiller's core beliefs. The company's Annual Report for 2000 states, "In fiscal year 2000, Green Mountain adopted the Appreciative Inquiry (AI) method of business analysis, which incorporates a highly positive, inclusive, and people-centered way of considering business development." Given his commitment to creating the conditions for people to be involved in an active and engaged way, Stiller says his experience with the Appreciative Inquiry process was a high point for him. The process "helped people explore what worked for them in the past and rekindle the excitement they felt in order to mobilize energy for the future."

If you make appreciation part of the culture, Stiller believes, "it's something that people do automatically. Whenever we approach any task, any new program, we ask, 'When have we seen examples of something like this working in the past? What is it that works? What is it about the way people were engaged with each other that made it work? How do we build on the principles we've extracted from our understanding of how things work well to approach this new situation?'"

Recently, for instance, the people planning the company's annual meeting explored the issue of what had made the previous year's meeting successful. They spoke with those involved the year before and reflected on the process and the results. This is what the planners found that had worked:

- Employees had a chance to meet and speak with people representing different layers and areas of the company.
- Critical ideas and points were conveyed through stories.
- The meeting was interactive rather than a talking-heads display.
- The company had carried the work from the prior year's meeting forward.

Employees not only evaluated what was successful at the prior meeting, but also recognized how the work they had done at the previous year's meeting influenced how things had gone in the company over the past 12 months.

Positive Image/Positive Action—The Vision

Bob uses *Namaste*, a Hindu greeting, which means, "May the God in you meet the God in me and together we are one," to describe his philosophy of positive imagery leading to positive action. "We are working towards one outcome rather than my way or your way," he says. "We have *our* way…understanding at the highest level, synergy rather than one way or another."

As the number of players in the specialty coffee world was declining and the size of individual companies was increasing, Green Mountain faced a challenge: to compete, the company had to decrease its cost of production and become more profitable. So it looked at its business processes, asking how each process could become more efficient. How could it reduce the cost of marketing by one or two cents per pound, for example? Every function of the company examined where and how it could tighten its belt. Cross-functional process teams examined it. Everybody took responsibility for tightening procedures. They made a target of decreasing their cost per pound of coffee by 25 cents. Many of the teams achieved their target. The result? Profitability soared, and so did the stock price.

"There was a trust relationship in the group," Stiller says. "Everyone seemed to know that they were trying to achieve the best possible solution for the group. There was tremendous give and take. Everyone was going to have to give something up to get something; there was a commitment to keep working it until we got to the right model."

Bob believes deeply in the power of the imagination. "When we aspire to something and trust the process, we may not be conscious of a synchronicity, but it is there. Like with the AI process, if we all keep the goal in mind, then something happens. Everything is happening in relationship to that goal. A clear shared goal, a sense of purpose, a sense of trust in the whole, and a full engagement of people with the support they need to act, helps sustain people's positive images of the future." So, Stiller strives to align the company's culture with employees' clear positive images of where they are going. "The organization's intention—the culture," he says, "is what happens when no one is around. The culture must fully leverage people."

Many years ago, one of Stiller's customer care managers kept a photograph of phone representatives for a large telemarketing group on the wall above her desk. She used it to help her focus on her own goals to grow her department of three. Stiller notes, "Today her department is bigger than the one in the photo."

Bob believes in the power of positive intentions and wants that to be recognized and known about him. "Having people know that about me helps me know it about myself and sustain it," he says. "It helps me be conscientious with other people." So GMCR takes approaches that help people believe in and support their positive intentions. It has many policies, practices, and rituals that nurture appreciative relationships and positive intentions.

Inevitably, though, differences arise when one works with other employees, especially members of one's team. How does Bob Stiller talk about those differences with his team members? How does he resolve the differences? Bob understands both the challenge and the gift of speaking with people in a way that is timely, works through the different perspectives, and reaches a common understanding. He schedules regular time with each of his staff and board members to enable this process and keep communication fresh and open.

Inquiry Inspired Action

Stiller speaks from experience when he talks about the energy ignited when people inquire into what works. He sees inquiry as a way of rolling different perspectives into a common vision while preserving the distinctive qualities of those perspectives. He believes that inquiry constructs an outcome that has energy because it joins the views of all involved. "The vision of each becomes the vision of all."

He saw examples of how inquiry inspired action in a whole-system initiative for business process improvement at GMCR. Employees inquired into issues such as "customer intimacy," "everyday faster, better, cheaper," and "excellence in execution." In doing so, they rediscovered and redesigned the business processes of market to sell, procure to pay, and order to cash.

They also told stories. One story, about customer intimacy, concerned a couple who traveled from Florida to Vermont every year to watch the leaves change colors in the fall. One year they called the company to order coffee, but said they couldn't make it up to Vermont because the husband was ill. So the customer service representative handling the call sent them a letter and enclosed leaves of different colors along with their coffee.

Pursuing inquiry into what works now permeates how the CEO interacts with the Green Mountain board, how people handle performance evaluations, even how they conduct meetings. They ask, "What will make this meeting successful, and what can we do to make it so?"

You might not pick Stiller out in a crowd. He has a modest presence. He meditates once or twice a day. He's shy. He speaks softly. He does not draw attention to himself. But if you speak with him and see him in action, you come to know who he is and how he leads his organization. You see that he is more interested in *creating the conditions* to support the culture he inspires than in spending time talking about it. He is interested in fostering a business that does good in the world, keeps people employed and happy, and continues to grow into an ever more successful enterprise.

Interview With Margaret Crawford

Margaret Crawford, Director-Human Resources, Harley-Davidson Motor Company, Milwaukee, Wisconsin

Kristine Crowell

Margaret Crawford attended the University of Wisconsin, Parkside, earning Business Management and Labor Economics degrees. She also graduated from Northwestern's Kellogg Graduate School of Management. In 1988, she joined Harley-Davidson as Manager of Staffing and became a Director of Human Resources. She is currently a Senior Vice President for Fortis Health.

I first met Margaret Crawford while interviewing for a position with Harley-Davidson. I could immediately sense that she was a warm, open, and non-judgmental person. I remember her eye contact the most. She wanted to hear more than the words I was saying; I felt she understood what listening was at a much deeper level. The questions she asked made me feel as if she were simply interested in getting to know me. She didn't approach the interview process as if I had to "sell" myself to her. She really just wanted to discuss our shared vision about change management. As she talked, I was drawn in by her soft-spokenness and confident articulation of her thoughts. I heard her use words that sparked passion in me: vision, strategy, commitment. Her leadership philosophy clearly was built around people being the key component to the success of an organization.

Meeting Margaret Crawford, for me, was what she would call a "defining moment." I now knew what the theme of my next chapter in life would be. It would include Crawford's vision of an Organizational Effectiveness group consisting of change management, career development, organizational development, and leadership development. I learned that integrity and honesty are at the core of her beliefs. Humility, graciousness, and reverence define her for me. You'll get to know Margaret Crawford more as you read through her quotes, stories, and insights.

The Task of Bringing out the Best in Human Beings and Organizations

Crawford spoke about how the five Harley-Davidson values are requirements for bringing out the best in people: tell the truth; be fair; keep your promises; respect the individual; and encourage intellectual curiosity. Telling the truth has to do with honesty, not just saying what someone wants to hear. Honest communication takes a lot of time. It requires a lot of questions, openness, and hearing the other person's perspective.

Margaret shared her belief that respecting the individual involves the ability to listen non-judgmentally. This lays the foundation for creating trust and peak experiences. "It's important to create an environment where the relationship building that optimizes performance on an individual level becomes behavior that's reinforced in the group and then in the organization." From an organizational perspective, in order to achieve Harley-Davidson's vision and goals, Crawford spoke about how individuals must focus on people's strengths, learn together, consider different perspectives—and definitely have fun. She also emphasized the importance of saying "thank you," which she says is a little thing: "It is such an easy gift, such a simple gift, and a powerful gift, but people sometimes just forget how important that really is."

Crawford looks for what she calls the "sweet spot," which in any relationship is about mutual benefit. What she means by that is, "Where does the overlap exist between people? That overlap between people, and among people and organizations, is the 'sweet spot' How can all benefit from the relationship?" It entails understanding individual and collective motivation, goals, and aspirations. She encourages people to look for this overlap in order to determine what it is people are interested in attaining and where the company can also attain its goals. This carries over to any relationship within the organization, including those with the employee, the shareholder, the community, and the government. The sweet spot becomes a powerful building block to success. It's also a means for developing a common vision and direction. What is in it for each person? Where is the nature of the mutually beneficial relationship? How does it translate into creating a future and common goals? That vision entails participation on the part of the group and/or the organization.

Appreciative Relationships

Feedback-rich environments are developed by allowing enough time for relationships to form. Sometimes groups get together and become very focused on getting the task done. They become more concerned about the immediate outcome rather than spending time learning about one another and jointly developing a common vision. However, Crawford has experienced that, with more time, people really begin to connect with a broader vision and understand the different components that make up that task. Yet she emphasizes that many people want to contribute and establish relationships, which require building communication skills and developing common "mental models." This creates a safe environment where people are comfortable providing feedback. It also results in people knowing that they are going to be heard and respected for what they bring to the table.

One example of how Margaret connects with people is her working relationship with a Harley-Davidson engineer. The engineer is very bright, analytical, and detail oriented, whereas Crawford has the tendency to be very inspirational and more "big picture." Their backgrounds are different. She explained to me how they use one another to balance each other out. "He's my reality check. I'm guaranteed that he will always look at things differently than I do," she says. They really enjoy each other's company because they know each will get an entirely different perspective. She confesses, "Why didn't I think of that!" And he'll say the same thing. She has 180 degrees covered and he has the other 180 degrees covered!

According to Crawford, "When we can talk about difficult topics with our colleagues, group, or team, it results in a better outcome and contributes to better decision-making. It's less expensive if you head the problem off earlier." She says, "I think that the authenticity or the honesty has to come from being able to confront and not to avoid or deny; that's where the realness comes in. We need to uplift the positive and be a visionary, but also be realistic and confrontational. They almost seem like they're opposite ends of the spectrum, yet all those components have to be present for authentic, appreciative, and accepting relationships."

Positive Image and Positive Action = Vision

How we view an initiative or project has quite a bit to do with our vision. "Sometimes people are limited by their own needs, wants, and motivations, whether it be by their own career aspirations, their income earning potential, or by their family or work group. I try to help people focus or to see an outcome larger than themselves. If you are looking at a horizon you can only see the farmland or the vista. It is imagining beyond what the eye can see. It is a function of the heart, head, and body and putting it all together to see the greater good." Margaret Crawford believes our visions should be broader in scope, consider all stakeholders and leverage potential business value. She sites an example when the scope of a career development initiative was defined primarily as a software implementation. Some software was bought that was supposed to be "implemented" in a short period of time. "This was not about just getting a system in place, it was about really making organizational change," Crawford clarified. "When Harley-Davidson invests in a system like this, it's not just to just save time and be efficient, but to make changes in how people are contributing their talents in the workplace. They can shorten the amount of time it takes people to get ready for new assignments and also cut the cost of recruitment and raise the level of job satisfaction." This was the vision.

Crawford continues to explain, "In order to get people's attention we need to look at the vision, what we want to realize, what's the objective, and what's the greater good. The vision creates an umbrella that encompasses all of the people that we're trying to influence. We thought about that from a broader perspective, and in my mind the purpose of that program was to create peak working experiences for our employees while realizing company objectives."

Margaret Crawford has an exceptional ability to see a larger outcome and get to the heart of the greater good. This is her compass. She shares some of her passion: "To have people go home at night where they can say, 'Man, I have learned so much, I am having so much fun, I am contributing, I know exactly what I'm supposed to be doing, I'm growing because of the different people that I'm interacting with, and I'm so engaged with what's really important to the business.' To have people be that pumped up knowing they wouldn't be bored when they came to work the next day—what a gift. Imagine how much potential would be unleashed."

Margaret shared with me that she was always moving on to the next job in her younger years: "I wanted to really establish myself as a professional, wanting to manage people in order to get more money, more status, and more influence in the organization." That perspective has changed in her life. She discovered that the common denominator for her really was "challenge." She views herself, not so much in the act of doing her job, but more in the process of learning and being involved in engaging new initiatives. That is how she defines challenge. Her greatest reward is multiplying what she knows through other people. "It has to do with passing along what I've learned. Then that will be perpetuated through their interactions with other people," she said insightfully. Her next challenge is figuring out how she can have more of an impact on people's lives in a much broader context.

Margaret Crawford's visionary leadership is a catalyst for successfully producing organizational change. "When working with the Information Services Management Council, one of the ways I got them engaged was for them to think about a peak career experience and to share it with the group. They had to go back in their history and find a time when they felt really passionate about their work and were having a lot of fun. As we went around the room, each person was asked to describe a situation. Those stories made it real for everyone." She then asked them, "Wouldn't that be great if you could have that feeling every day? And not just you, but everyone that works for you and for the company? And how about everyone involved with Harley-Davidson?"

Crawford felt that in order to recreate peak experiences, she had to start with them, so people could feel them, taste them, know what they're about, and think back in their memory when they were at that point. You can start to figure out what needs to be done to change the current mindset and to get people excited about moving toward the vision. "This is an example," Crawford explains, "of how you can look at a project as just getting the software in, or how can you change the organization with a vision that is much broader and contributing to creating peak experiences for people."

Margaret believes one must look at the past, present, and future for positive images. It seems very simple. Considering the past, it's a combination of what people realize about the state of the world and the learnings they've had. The creativity really occurs in the present. People begin to see connections between seemingly disparate events or thoughts, which create images that weren't previously thought about. Then, given the past, determine what the organization is good at and what they can get excited about with those creative connections.

On a very personal level, Margaret shared with me how she creates positive images for herself. These images help her create the life she wants to live. One image she shared with me was of her home. With all her openness, she began to tell me how she creates this life. "You might wonder how my home is a vision for me. Some people view their home as a show place, like having a home right out of a decorating magazine. My home represents a place where my children would want to come back to and where friends would want to stay because there's enough room. Everyone would enjoy good food and feel comfortable. I would have a lot of personal, beautiful things that I enjoy in my life as a part of my home. That is the feeling I want to create. I've been pretty successful at doing that as a result of having that vision."

The Spirit of Inquiry

Margaret Crawford epitomizes humility. She replaces the leadership role of telling and knowing with really listening and teaching. She never professes to be all-knowing. "Inquiry lives in me from a basic insecurity of not having the answers. I think that most people have that insecurity and some people fight [throughout] their whole lives trying to hide the lack of knowledge, especially now as the world becomes more complex." She feels that her ability to really inquire, listen, and teach has something to do with her gender and her ethnicity. When she began her career, the only way Crawford was able to work effectively with groups of men was not to buck heads with them. She often admitted when she didn't know something and asked a lot of questions. She learned a lot and acquired quite a bit of information!

Margaret inherently creates a climate that is open to sharing diverse ideas and in which people want to learn from one another. In order to replicate the learning, from a group perspective, she recommends an after-action-review. "Here we take a look at the goal and then the experience. We have the members of the group share their experiences on what they learned and what they could have done differently. We don't approach it from a critical or performance perspective, but in the spirit of trying to learn from it and to take those learnings and apply them to future situations." Crawford believes, "More prized are the characteristics or qualities of leaders that create an environment where curiosity and a willingness to ask questions and explore are valued."

When Crawford traced where she developed her "spirit of inquiry," she talked about her ethnicity.

I am a third generation Japanese-American. I think that tribal mores and customs, even though my Dad grew up in L.A. and my Mom in Maui, were perpetuated. In fact, I have been amazed to meet other Japanese-Americans and find that their way of expressing, in terms of the cadence of the speech and ways of thinking, are very similar to mine even though I didn't grow up in a Japanese community. I think that says something about the perpetuation of family values, not in all cases, but certainly in my case. So the ways of interacting, this idea of asking questions and listening as opposed to dictating, are natural for me.

The Role of Positive Affect in Bringing out the Best

When Margaret Crawford was considering working for Harley-Davidson in the late eighties, she interviewed with John Campbell, Vice President of Human Resources. Campbell inspired Crawford. She felt that he really had a lot of compassion for the working person, not just the executive. He had a vision of creating a different kind of workplace. He wanted to do more partnering with the unions and wanted employees to have a say on how work would get done. This was progressive thinking at the time. He really understood what the soul of the company was about. "That was a defining moment for me because it was a time when I was ready to take on more managerial responsibility," Crawford shared. This decision had some risk associated with it because Harley had recently filed for bankruptcy, the buildings were deteriorating, and many people were laid off. Despite the risk, Crawford had a sense that Campbell was somebody she knew she'd love to work for. "If it didn't work out I could have always found something else, but I just had a sense that working for John Campbell and Harley-Davidson was the right thing to do," she explained.

Camaraderie plays a very important role in positively effecting change in organizations. Harley-Davidson is a company that is based on relationships. Sometimes unfortunate events bring a work group together. People provide a level of support for each other. When you share time together and work closely it can bring out feelings of hope, inspiration, joy, and confidence. These feelings create camaraderie, a word that has a deep meaning for Crawford. "An organization is a lot more than a corporate entity; it has to do with the spirit of the people that are affiliated with it and their sense of obligation and responsibility. Whether it be protecting the brand or making Harley a good place to work, this is what has contributed to our success and Harley-Davidson's success."

Crawford emphasizes the importance of congruence between her leadership philosophy and her leadership-in-action. This congruence shapes the choices she makes. From her perspective, one of the most valuable and essential leadership qualities has to do with integrity. She explains,

44

It's not just saying what you really mean, but it has to do with leading a life that fits with your values of what you say. It comes from my experience with leaders. I developed my leadership philosophy from observation. I think some people are inspiring and know how to create an environment where there is a lot of hope, inspiration, and camaraderie. It comes from a certain set of qualities a person has. It doesn't matter what organization it is; integrity is key. Integrity has to do with congruence with what people say they are about, their belief system, and how they live. I look for people who have that kind of integrity.

By learning from many defining moments, Crawford has internalized her philosophy as, "passion around seeking the greater good, integrity, perpetuating leadership, and having a willingness to change." She believes that unless you're able to sustain a level of excitement, interest, urgency, focus, and learning, then it's not even worth getting involved. "You can't be all things to all people. So you might as well pick the things that you really want to commit to. Otherwise, don't even get involved."

She's also learned to compromise. "Seek out people with different perspectives. It's the people with different perspectives that you learn the most from. Ask yourself, what can I learn from this person? By being open to living vicariously through others, you'll widen the experiences of your own life and expand your own contributions."

Listen, Listen, Listen

**Michael J. P. Burns, Vice President - Human Resources,
Richard M. Pellett, Vice President and General Manager,
both of Hunter Douglas Window Fashions Division,
Broomfield, Colorado**

Amanda Trosten-Bloom

*Michael J. P. (Mike) Burns is Vice President - Human Resources,
and Richard M. (Rick) Pellett is Vice President and General
Manager, for Hunter Douglas Window Fashions Division in
Broomfield, Colorado. Together, Mike and Rick served as "spiritual
leaders" and champions of Focus 2000—a whole-system
appreciative inquiry for culture transformation. Since that time,
they have continued to apply Appreciative Inquiry to their everyday
business and leadership in such areas a strategic planning, business
process improvement, and organization design.*

There's no better view than from a west-facing window in
Hunter Douglas Window Fashions Division's administrative
building. You can see the reflection of the sunrise against the purple
mountains of Colorado's Front Range, or watch the sun dip slowly
behind some of the nation's tallest peaks. It's a scene worth
noticing—both an inspiration to and a reflection of two of the leaders
in this remarkable organization.

In the late 1980's, Hunter Douglas Window Fashions Division
was still trying to discover itself. Formed through an international
company's acquisition of an entrepreneurial organization called
Thermal Technology, the Division manufactured and marketed
"Duette honeycomb shades"—a unique variation of window
covering that combined form (soft, durable fabric/thin stack) with
function (state-of-the-art insulation). While highly functional and
energy efficient, Duette shades were also successfully promoted
as fashion for the home: stylistically and aesthetically appealing
window treatments for the upscale consumer. This was a

revolutionary step for the industry, which previously marketed its products based almost exclusively on their functionality.

As a result, Duette shades achieved unprecedented success and renewed consumer interest in window coverings in an industry that hadn't had a significant new product introduction in decades. Retail sales soared to an estimated $300 million by 1988. In 2001, the Duette honeycomb shade remains one of the biggest brands in the custom window coverings market, second only to other brands that were later released by the same Division.

Explosive sales led to explosive growth. The Division turned over three General Managers in a mere 18 months, and then one "stuck"—thus planting the seeds for today's Division. This new General Manager began hiring in outside professionals to help grow the fledgling organization. Two of these outside leaders—Rick Pellett and Mike Burns—would eventually lead a spiritual rejuvenation of a much-changed organization. But that's a story yet to come.

Meanwhile, back in the early 1980's, they joined Hunter Douglas within a year of one another. Pellett was retained as the Division's first Controller, later to become Chief Financial Officer and General Manager. Burns, the self-named "HR weanie," began a human resources function out of nothing, eventually becoming Vice President of a mid-sized and highly professional department, whose organizational impact is significant and growing.

Pellett's first week on the job foreshadowed the rest of his tenure in which he would perpetually be called to imagine and construct new strategies and systems, new ways of looking at things. As he describes it, on his first day he was asked to prepare a budget. "How long do I have?" he asked.

"One week."

"Who should I go to for information?"

"Hurley," he was told. But Hurley, then Operations Manager, now President of the HD North America Manufacturing group, had been there for only three days. Pellett grabbed his stack of green ledger sheets and got to work, diligently doing his part to create the stable leadership and professional systems that are now second nature to the Division and the Company.

Burns's beginnings were equally, but differently, challenging. When he came to work for Hunter Douglas, it had 65 employees, no human resources systems, and a merely intuitive concept of professional leadership. He remembers,

Small as it was, the Company kept pushing me - and encouraged me to push back. I'm *still* pushing back. That means a lot to me. I stayed—*kept on staying*—because I could see I was making a difference. Now, thirteen years later, I'm seeing the results of some of what I'd hoped for early on, but I'm still not finished. As long as our visions for the organization keep growing like they have, I intend to keep on playing.

Even at the time they joined the Division, Pellett and Burns were unlikely partners: tall and short; introverted and extraverted; linear and intuitive minds. Nobody would have guessed that they would join together as one—that they would, together, become conscience, gadfly, and prophet to both the Division and the larger North American organization. No one would have seen that they would have become one another's closest ally, friend, and teacher. No one would have imagined them as co-champions of some of the more innovative cultural and strategic work that the Division had ever seen.

These are Rick Pellett's and Mike Burns's stories. They're stories of individual values that can make enormous ripples in organizations and communities. They're stories of tenacity and of the miracles that can be created when attention is given over time. They're stories of how people can accomplish great things if they will trust in "other" ways of knowing. Last but not least, they're stories of the transformational power of listening.

The Task of Bringing out the Best in Human Beings and Organizations

For a four-year period, Burns and Pellett worked together to conceive of and implement a culture transformation process that would engage, involve, and grow employees. This landmark intervention took the Division from dwindling employee satisfaction scores in 1997, to an emphasis on employee education and development that in 2001 employees describe as "the best I've ever seen." Where did they learn to do work this way?

Twenty years ago, Mike Burns worked in a management position for an engineering company. The company hired a new boss for him, a man who was, as Burns describes him, "brilliant, but without a political clue." This boss got to know Burns, and came to understand the skills he brought. He used him as a resource, asked his advice, and generally tapped into what he did best. He allowed himself to imagine possibilities, and then let Burns help him figure out how to put flesh on the plans. "I got to do what I did well, and so did he. We were a great team. He taught me about partnership, about using other people's skills when you need them, so that you could pay attention to what you did really well."

But letting people do what they do well was only *part* of the lesson that Burns took from that organization. He soon learned to pay attention not just to what people do well, but also to what they *like*. At some point, Mike was offered a sales position with this same company: great position; great money; lots of travel. But full-time travel wasn't what Burns wanted with a young family at home, so he turned it down. A year later, when a senior human resources position opened up, using many of the same skills for which Burns had demonstrated both ability and passion, the same manager came back to Mike and offered him the job. "He'd gotten to know me," reflects Burns. "He encouraged me to concentrate on what I did best, and it brought me to life. I felt engaged, enriched, and enlivened by doing what I really wanted to do, in a way that worked for my *whole* life—not just my work life."

Rick Pellett described similarly "finding" himself under the leadership of an ex-boss. "Joe believed in developing talent, and he gave people opportunities to step out of their niches. I was the Controller—but he sent me to trade shows. What good could I contribute at a trade show? Nothing, really, but it helped me to understand the business better." As Pellett described this experience, he reflected on how it contrasted with other organizations he'd worked for.

Before that, I'd worked in organizations where the head guy was the head guy, and I just executed. In this

49

organization, I was never told, 'This isn't your area.' Instead, I was encouraged to learn whatever I could, so that I could think and act bigger. Sometimes I wish I could work for Joe again. Because with all the knowledge I've picked up since then, I could be making a greater contribution to that business than I did at the time.

Pellett and Burns reflect with pride on the ways in which they've passed on some of the respect, the trust, and the mentorship they received to one of their co-workers in today's Hunter Douglas. Mary Beth was Manager of Human Resources and "sharp as a tack." She wanted to move into the Operations part of the business. She approached Rick and Mike for support and coaching. They helped her think through what she was looking for, and what she'd need to make it happen. They made collective agreements: she would attend a few outside classes and workshops that focused on skills that they knew she would need in her new position, and Pellett and Burns would find a place for her where she could stretch and grow with support.

Within a year, Pellett says,

We found the job. It was a stretch, but it wasn't over her head. It was a place where she could succeed, and where the risk we were all taking was a good, calculated, one. That risk has already paid off big time. She's brought more depth to her work in Operations for having known another life before—and she's also gotten solid mentoring and experience that will help her to *give back* in the future, some of what she's been given. I know that Mary Beth will be a great contributor to this organization for a very long time.

Several people in the Window Fashions Division have similar stories of having been trained, cross-trained, and supported in stretching into new roles that more fully suited their natures and interests. Pellett, Burns, and other leaders have consistently "walked their talk," in terms of bringing out the best in individuals within the organization. But making a difference one person at a time wasn't enough for this leadership team. It wasn't enough to simply provide opportunities for high fliers or for people who had self-identified as wanting or needing new or different challenges. They chose to approach "bringing out the best" on a more *systemic* basis. Three years ago, they grabbed on to and supported a grassroots effort to create Hunter Douglas University (HDU)—at the time a virtual university, eventually to become an actual Corporate Learning Center.

Back in 1999, when the Division first broke ground on HDU, it was designed as a training, learning, and meeting place: multiple conference rooms, a library, a computer lab, and two, large, connected classrooms equipped for meetings of 100+ people. It came to include a career resource center, including a full-time Career Planning/Communications professional, and a gathering place for numerous personal as well as professional development activities. "HDU has had a tremendous lifting effect on the organization," says Pellett. "It lets people know that we value them. But more important, it gives people a way to learn new skills, to master new ways of working that eventually benefit both them and the organization."

Appreciative Relationships

In exploring their experiences, both Mike Burns and Rick Pellett had lots to say about the role of appreciative relationships in creating an effective, positive organization. They seemed to agree that mutual openness and honesty was one—but only one—way of promoting those types of relationships. What seemed equally important to them was providing a mirror by which people could see themselves and others in a larger context. "Keep talking about people's achievements and successes," says Burns. "Thank people publicly when they do something right or go the extra mile. If you don't put that in the spotlight, it eventually grows dimmer."

Pellett says this type of acknowledgment has an effect both on the receiver *and* the giver. "It's easy to build trust and respect with someone who you intuitively believe is smart or effective—someone whose values and contributions are similar to, or at least compatible, with your own." But, he said,

51

Where things get hard is when someone's *really different*. When they think differently or act differently from ways that you've been trained and conditioned to respect. In cases like that, it helps me to publicly acknowledge what is there—to pay attention to the value that that person adds . . . the contribution that they make. It trains me to see the bigger picture, even as it builds their sense of trust. It creates an environment that makes it easier for everyone to speak their minds and contribute, when it comes time to make big and complicated decisions.

As is true with their philosophy of "bringing out the best," Mike and Rick have worked to incorporate appreciative relationships into the fabric—the systems—of the organization. Four years ago, they and other leaders in the organization established what they call a "whole-system strategic and business planning process." Believing that many ideas are always better than one, they engage up to 150 people, from all levels of the organization, sometimes including customers and suppliers, in their annual look at the business. "This practice is important for several reasons," reflects Pellett. "It elevates people's thinking and helps them to place their work in the larger context of the organization and the industry. It signals that we appreciate people and what they contribute. Finally, it demonstrates that everyone's ideas will be accepted, respected, and used by the company. I feel really proud of what we've accomplished in the area of participation."

Positive Image/Positive Action and the Spirit of Inquiry

"Where do this organization's positive images of the future come from?" I asked, as we sat looking at those spectacular mountains. "Anywhere and everywhere," replied Mike. "When you tap into people's innermost thoughts and dreams, their best recollections, their visions and aspirations . . . when you start asking questions about those things, the positive images start to *bounce back*." As he later reflected, the challenge is to capture the images that emerge, and then provide support for the momentum the images create. Otherwise, you just end up with happy images and no action.

Once again, the systemic nature of "positive image/positive action" and "the spirit of inquiry" becomes clear as Pellett and Burns describe their organizational practices. When we're at our best, our leadership team brings different people together whenever something needs to be done, people with a variety of skills and interests. We ask them how to make things better. We give them space and time to think and act. We encourage them to think and act differently—to question the status quo—to take us to new places. As a result of asking these kinds of questions, people from production and administration, line and staff, have frequently joined together to create new systems and processes that have radically enhanced the business.

Take the problem they were facing years ago: Frequent mandatory overtime. Groups of people from all around the Division worked within their business units to consider what might be and to come up with customized solutions. These new solutions included: streamlining of the work; flexible or adapted work schedules; and ongoing solicitation of volunteers. The result? No more mandatory overtime, division-wide flexible time, and work-at-home options for a broad base of administrative employees.

The Role of Positive Affect in Bringing out the Best

Providing opportunities for positive images to emerge through inquiry is critical, though not everything. Positive—even *intimate*—relationships are also fertile ground on which positive images of the future can grow. As an example, Rick recalled having been part of a "Cinderella" baseball team when he was a kid, playing Little League on Coronado Island in California. Though a quirk of fate had the team playing an extra playoff game, and though there were moments in which the games looked pretty grim, Pellett said, "I *knew* we were going to win. I knew how well we knew each other. Heck, we lived on an island and did *everything* together! We'd spent all this time working, and I knew how committed we were. I knew that we had clicked. I simply allowed myself *to know* we would win."

Mike Burns's story also reflected the role of intimate relationships in the formation of positive images of the future. He

53

learned through experience with his family that when you value good relationships over short-term gain, the long-term results are more positive.

I had a job offer back in Philadelphia. It was right after we'd moved from there to Denver, and I figured it was a great opportunity to get back to where we'd come from. I came home and announced that we were moving back. Everyone in my family—my wife and all three of my small children—all looked at me, waved their hands, and said, "Bye, bye!" Just like that! I thought, "Uh-oh . . . guess I'd better rethink that one." The next day I started looking for a local job. It's how I came to Hunter Douglas. I took a cut in pay in order to come here but it was worth it, given how the rest of my family felt about staying. Imagine if I'd just plowed ahead and insisted on having "my way"! I've never forgotten that lesson. Big decisions and changes are a "together" kind of thing. You just can't make good decisions without good relationships.

The effect of camaraderie and positive affect in the workplace is evident in the recent development of the HR function under Burns. Late last year, a new Human Resources Manager joined the department. She initiated monthly gatherings for the group: times to play together, not just work. One month they had an off-site birthday celebration, another, a baby shower. They held the gatherings at people's homes, and everyone brought potluck dishes to share. "Morale has never been higher in the group," says Burns. "But more important, neither has performance. The trust and respect and growing intimacy within the group has spilled over into the day-to-day. People who rarely used to speak up or share ideas are now regularly coming forward with solutions. It just goes to show that when you engage the whole person, the whole person becomes willing to contribute."

Words of Wisdom to Pass Along

As we concluded our interviews, I asked Burns and Pellett to share any closing words of wisdom—things that they'd wished they'd learned earlier, lessons that they wanted to impart to the next generation of leaders behind them.

"Listen, listen, listen!" responded Burns. "I always had the answers and told people what they had to do. It took me years to understand that listening to people is your key to success—and your key to *their* success."

"Surround yourself with people who are different," echoes Pellett. "Listen to people and try to see the world the way they see it - different values and all. Years ago I'd have been a much better leader if I'd understood that differences in how people think are of great value, rather than a deterrent to a quality process."

"Oh, yes—one more thing," says Mike Burns. "Don't try to 'fix' yourself or other people. Just figure out a way to work around people's weaknesses and play to their strengths. If someone's not good at something—whatever you do—don't sweat it. Just find a way to get it done that's consistent with their nature."

Communications - More Than Just Part Of This Company's Name

Ricky Lewis, Manager-Real Estate Operations, South/ Virginia, Verizon Communications, Durham, North Carolina

Christopher Flaugh

Ricky Lewis is Manager of the Real Estate Operations for Verizon's South/Virginia area. He and his staff of 60 manage 1,200+ administrative buildings and network facilities in six states and have been part of a company-wide GTE Appreciative Inquiry process. A recent Verizon Gold Circle winner, Ricky has been with the company 28 years. He and his family live in Durham, North Carolina.

Founded in 1918 as the Richland Center Telephone Company that covered five telephone exchanges in rural Wisconsin, GTE grew over the years to become one of the nation's largest local and long distance telephone service providers. Following the 2000 merger with Bell Atlantic, the new company, Verizon, emerged as one of the world's leading providers of communications services. Verizon companies are the largest providers of wireline and wireless communications in the United States, with nearly 109 million access line equivalents and more than 27.5 million wireless customers. Verizon is also the world's largest provider of print and online directory information, a Fortune 10 company with approximately 260,000 employees and more than $63 billion in annual revenues. Verizon's global presence extends to 40 countries in the Americas, Europe, Asia, and the Pacific.

Verizon Communications' South Region headquarters building in Durham, NC is an interesting study in contrasts. The stately façade of the main building is reminiscent of a Civil War-era plantation, but the interior contains over 160,000 square feet of modern, professional workspace. This is a very appropriate setting for Ricky Lewis who, much like the building itself, exudes a sense of stability, solidity, and almost serenity, yet is thoroughly equipped for success in today's marketplace. Joining the GTE organization in 1973, Ricky Lewis has progressed through a series of increasingly responsible management roles and corporate mergers, such as GTE/Contel and GTE/Bell Atlantic.

The Task of Bringing out the Best in Human Beings and Organizations

When Lewis began his tenure at GTE in 1973, he felt he was perceived as different in the organization because he was both a racial minority and a recent college graduate without "real world" experience. Recognizing the possible uneasiness that Lewis might be facing, his supervisor gave him an opportunity to enhance his expertise in the area of electrical design, and thus become the subject matter expert for his work group. This enabled Lewis to make a greater short-term contribution to the organization but, more important, this also inspired greater confidence in his own abilities.

In an unrelated situation, this same supervisor had received complaints about a job Lewis was managing. However, before acting, Lewis's supervisor accompanied him to the jobsite, viewed the areas of concern, clearly expressed that he was very pleased with the work performed, and let the complainant know that this was a very difficult job situation which required more support and assistance for Lewis, rather than complaints against him. Lewis recalled, "Possibly more than anything else, his expressed confidence in me boosted my own confidence in myself and probably had a big impact on my future success within GTE."

Following this example, Lewis has consistently used a similar approach to bring out the best in his own employees. In one such example, a relatively new employee in his group had not been performing up to expectations. Believing that this individual possessed the skills and abilities necessary for success, Lewis assigned him a special project, explaining the project's critical nature, high visibility, and compressed time frame. While initially it may have seemed risky to his colleagues to entrust such a high profile project to an unproven employee, the project was completed on schedule, within budget, and to the satisfaction of all involved.

Frequent progress reports initiated by the employee served not only as status updates, but also assured Lewis that his confidence in this individual was justified.

Confidence and communication have been the keys to bringing out the best, as Lewis summarizes,

Individuals must see that you believe in them and their ability to perform. When you show that you have confidence in an individual, they will try harder to live up to that expectation. The same applies to groups and organizations. It's important to clearly communicate your expectations. Then show confidence in the group or organization to meet those expectations, with minimal interruptions by you.

Sounds simple enough: *Have confidence in others' ability to perform, communicate expectation levels, then stand back and allow them to live up to those expectations. This becomes a virtuous cycle of success as they then have confidence in others.*

Appreciative Relationships

Moving on to the topic of appreciative relationships, the importance of effective communications surfaced once again. Development of appreciative relationships throughout all levels of the organization has been enhanced through a series of staff meetings that have grown in size and scope. Years ago, staff meetings were for management staff only; it was the responsibility of managers to share information from the staff meeting with their employees. One of Lewis's first moves was to involve hourly employee representatives in these meetings. Later this participation grew to include all members of the organization, both management and hourly.

It hasn't always been an easy task to take all 60 employees away from the job for an entire day and bring them together from a six-state area, but the benefits derived have been well worth the effort. Employees know what is expected of them, what direction the organization is headed, and what their role is. They have the opportunity to express any concerns or questions and receive direct feedback. Sometimes the answer might be, "I don't know, but I will find out." That level of honesty is important in any relationship.

Ultimately, the fact that management takes the time and has the respect for employees to share openly the department's plans goes a long way towards strengthening those relationships. Recently, these meetings were expanded again to include all vendors and contractors who perform work for the department during the year.

Employee recognition is always on the agenda for these meetings. Verizon and Corporate Real Estate have a variety of employee recognition programs available, and Lewis has consistently made use of them much more extensively than any of his peers. Although Lewis's group represents roughly five per cent of the department's total headcount, they received 24 per cent of the department's employee recognition awards in 2000. During each meeting, Lewis takes the opportunity to present awards and recognize employees to the entire group. For Lewis's group, "Employee recognition is not an option; it is as important as the budget."

On a daily basis, open and honest communication is the rule throughout the department. "I try not to place any barriers on communication," says Lewis. "There is no protocol on who is allowed to call me directly. Although I encourage employees to work closely with and to communicate with their supervisors, I clearly acknowledge that I have an open door policy."

After 28 years with the company and experience dealing with mergers, Lewis's take on working through the often-tumultuous merger process is,

> With any merger there is bound to be change from what you have been previously accustomed to. That's life. However, with any change, at some point in time the change will become business as usual. In other words, rather than resisting or fighting against the merger, which is bound to occur anyhow, start working within the confines of the newly merged organization. Find confidence in the leadership of the decision makers, realizing that if you were in a position of being one of those decision makers, you too might be making the same choices.

So, Lewis's keys to developing appreciative relationships include: *open and honest communication throughout <u>all</u> levels of* the organization; seeking out frequent opportunities to express appreciation where it is due; and looking at things from another's perspective.

Positive Image and Positive Action

What about the power of positive thinking? What role does it play in our personal and professional lives? As in the children's story, *The Little Engine That Could*, if you think you can, you can. "Through this level of positive thinking, one is more willing to reach out for more opportunities, for more responsibilities, for more experience," says Lewis. "It's important to maintain that positive attitude to the point of being willing to take risks, and even fail at times. We find ourselves doing more of that these days, and that's not necessarily a bad thing."

The Role of Positive Affect in Bringing out the Best

We all follow our own, somewhat unique paths to bringing out the best in ourselves. Ricky Lewis's journey would look something like this:

I was fortunate enough to be hired into a company and into a department that I truly enjoy. I was then given the responsibility to perform and was allowed to make some mistakes along the way. Fortunately, I had the presence of mind to learn from those mistakes and to move on. I feel that I have been blessed to surround myself with people with whom I shared things in common, namely a strong work ethic and moral character. As I mentioned earlier, my big break came from not being fired from the company but, instead, being given a boost of confidence. From that point on, I have been in a position to take advantage of opportunities that have furthered my career within [Verizon].

A Few Final Words

Looking back on his career, Ricky had no regrets, but did indicate that he would have benefited from more mentoring early on. Keeping that in mind, it has been satisfying for him to pave the way for others to follow—to be their mentor. In his words, "I have always felt that a true leader is also a good follower. That is what I would tell others about leadership. If you really want to be a good leader, put yourself in the role of those who you wish to lead."

Chapter Three

Supporting Wellness

In this chapter, leaders in three organizations have similar values about wholeness of individuals and in communities. They tell stories about their leadership philosophy and the actions that lead to healthy staff members, organizations, and a healthy world. Mike Green, CEO of Concord Hospital in New Hampshire, gives glimpses of himself from his adolescent commitment to becoming a leader, to his organization's current collaborative methods. Dr. Sarah Eagger, a medical leader in several English organizations, reflects on how her deep spiritual base guides her leadership practices. As CEO of the Fetzer Institute, Dr. Thomas Inui demonstrates a consciousness in leading a foundation that believes: "The key to humanity's future lies in the productive linkage of the mind, body, and spirit."

Excellence And Caring:
Appreciative Leadership

Michael B. Green, President and CEO, Concord Hospital and Capital Region Health Care, Concord, New Hampshire

Joan E. Murray

President and CEO of Concord Hospital and Capital Region Health Care, Mike Green has been in health care management for over 20 years. A graduate of Dartmouth College and Sloan School of Management at MIT, Mike serves on the boards of several community organizations. Mike enjoys family time, and playing hockey and tennis.

> Care more than others think is wise
> Risk more than others think is safe
> Dream more than others think is practical
> Expect more than others think is possible
> -Anonymous

This quotation appears on the Concord Hospital "Success in Leadership" brochure.

Ice crystals flew through the air as Mike Green carved a sudden turn at the side of the net. He stopped a quick pass, whirled around, and slapped the puck into the corner, beating the goalie's defensive lunge and demonstrating his fast, intense style. "Nice play, Mike," people yelled. A smile lit up his face.

I had attended the 1992 hospital benefit hockey game hoping to see Mike Green, our new leader, play. As I watched his competitive, yet positive, energy on the ice, I had a feeling that exciting changes would be happening soon.

Mike Green is the President and CEO of Concord Hospital and Capital Region Health Care Corporation (CRHC) in New Hampshire. Over the past several years he has led our 180-bed not-for-profit community hospital through changes and difficulties, and also to great success. He's accomplished it all with integrity and caring, while encouraging us to strive toward a vision of excellence.

The Task of Bringing out the Best in Human Beings and Organizations

JM: I've worked at Concord Hospital for 19 years, first in the Clinical Laboratory and then in Organizational Development. There's been remarkable growth and achievement since you became our leader in 1992. How do you bring out the best in us?

MG: I think first it's a matter of trying to be positive, and supportive and encouraging of people, particularly when they do things well. Beyond that, there's the assessment of what people's strengths and weaknesses are. As part of mentoring people, you want to make sure they—themselves—understand what their strengths and weaknesses are. You want them to use their strengths to their optimum ability.

It's a matter of combinations of people. You try to make sure that you have a team that has the strengths and weaknesses in different areas, so you don't end up with a liability by everybody having a weakness in the same area. The team's success is very important, so again, you want to encourage and support that team success, and then people feel good about their contributions and they don't worry so much about their weaknesses.

JM: Can you share a story—a "high-point" moment in bringing out the best?

MG: When we went through the reduction in workforce it was a very traumatic time. From a business standpoint, from a mission standpoint, and from an accountability standpoint, it had to be done. But it was not something anyone wants to go through.

I think the team of people involved really rose to the challenge. A lot of organizations say, "Okay, a five percent cut across the board," because it's easy. Instead, we went through a department-by-department assessment: "Do we have a misalignment of our resources to our demand? Do we have an opportunity for systems improvement and to change the resource requirements?" And we did it in a team environment.

Multiple factors were really important. The individuals involved needed to feel that they weren't competing with each other to try and retain the most resources possible. They also needed to feel that they were each contributing to the aggregate. They needed to feel that their views and their perspectives were respected. We got through it, I think, about as successfully as any organization can get through something like that. There was a tremendous sense of doing what needed to be done, doing it in a thoughtful manner, doing it in a compassionate manner, and I think each individual felt like he or she contributed.

JM: The reduction in force in 1993 shook the organization, even though there was generous support for outplacements and "survivors." It must have involved difficult choices. As a leader, how did you help the team accomplish this?

MG: Well, we did it by recognizing the obvious, that we absolutely needed to make a change. I talked about respect, that no idea is a bad idea, and that we needed to explore a lot of things. The toughest aspect of the process was recognizing that, in all likelihood, it would cost one of the senior managers his or her job as well. We went through the process with a lot of integrity and achieved good outcomes.

JM: Who do you remember really appreciating you? What did they do?

MG: Usually it's people I've mentored in some way. If I think people have really good ideas and competencies, then I'm willing to push the envelope so they can take a risk. In an organization that was being challenged in terms of overall economic performance, I was still somewhat of an advocate. I said, "Even though we're very attentive to our resources now, let's try to allow this individual some latitude."

I also think it's been some combination of how I've supported them professionally and how I've supported them personally in times of need. I encourage people to always keep a balance between their personal and professional lives. If something personal is going on then that should take center stage, and the organization has to support them during that. I'm always embarrassed when people do remember me, but it feels good that people feel like I've been a friend, a boss, and a colleague.

Appreciative Relationships

JM: Soon after you came here, you moved your office from the administrative suite to a busy corridor and announced an "open door" policy. As you think about the role of appreciation at work, how have you developed a feedback-rich environment?

MG: I try to create such an environment by giving feedback, and trying to make it safe for people to give feedback to me. I try to be just Mike. If you see my door is open, come in. At hospital town meetings, everyone is encouraged to come, provide feedback, and ask questions.

From an organizational perspective, one way we've created a feedback-rich environment is through a team: the Chief Operating Officer, the Vice President of HR and the Director of Employee Assistance Programs. They do night rounds periodically, and go from floor to floor and sit and talk with staff. There is a feedback-rich environment and relationship between administration and the medical staff. As they've gotten to know members of senior management, physicians don't wait until a problem festers and is truly infected. They raise issues early on, which makes it much easier to fix before it gets serious.

JM: Do you think that one reason you have such a good relationship with the medical staff is the fact that your dad was a physician on staff at Concord Hospital?

MG: I don't know if it is because my father was a physician and I grew up knowing what the pressures of being a physician are, or whether it was because of the diversity of experiences I've had in my career, but I have a deep respect for physicians. If I really want to have good relationships with members of the medical staff, I have to be empathetic to their point of view. I have to listen to what they're saying from their role as physicians, and how changes at the hospital may affect their everyday lives.

When we redesigned what we do on patient care units, it really tested my relationship with the medical staff. What I had to do, from the standpoint of respect and appreciation, was to go to various medical departments. The department of surgery, for example, was very vocal: "We want to go back. We want things to be the way they used to be." I understood from their perspective, but I had to ask them, "Go back how far? Go back 6 months? Go back 6 years? Because nothing stays the same around here." I was respectful. I listened. I tried to be attentive to those things that we really needed to do to improve, and tried to be committed to a journey of change.

If I expect physicians to be appreciative of me, I have to be appreciative of them. It's a funny world. I think that there are some hospital administrators who don't get it. It's far better to try to find a way to be successful without undermining physicians' personal, financial, or professional objectives. And that creates an overall greater appreciation among us.

I think in hindsight, those physicians who are here really respect and appreciate the benefits that we have derived, as an organization, by continuing down that path of change. What that has done from the standpoint of creating a more appreciative environment, is that they're more willing to say, "I don't know if we can do that, but maybe this is worth talking about." It helps create an environment of flexibility.

JM: As part of Capital Region Health Care, our hospital continues to develop relationships with other hospitals and organizations. The CRHC often uses the image of a "bridge." For instance, the CRHC icon is a New England covered bridge and we call our shared Intranet "The Bridge." What advice can you give about "building bridges," about collaborating and merging?

MG: First of all, you have to focus on common interests. Before we enter into a partnership, we have open, honest discussions. We try to understand and see if there are enough shared culture, vision, and values, and also how cultural dissonance might impede success. We try to establish how our mutual interests can be served. For us to share a loaf of bread is better than one of us getting a full loaf and the other getting crumbs. The consequence of getting crumbs is that one party becomes bitter. We also try to figure out how to make the loaf bigger for all.

Positive Image and Positive Action
JM: I've heard you encourage exciting new ideas and projects, such as Cardiac Surgery and now the Cancer Center. Where and how do these dynamic and compelling positive images of the future arise?

MG: It's recognition that the future is most likely going to be different from the past. Then creative ideas emerge in anticipation of that future, and those ideas energize people to adapt to the future and to control their own destiny. If one accepts the notion that we can always improve, then that takes imagination, because it's about change.

Cardiac Surgery is a good case to show that creativity goes along with the excellence of what we're doing. It has to do with the cardiologists, the anesthesiologists, the intensivists, the caliber of nursing staff, and a myriad of other factors. The passion was around trying to take care of our cardiac patients in a way as close to optimal as possible. The outcome was the Cardiac Surgery program. It created a lot of mutual appreciation among all the professionals, the community, and the patients receiving cardiac services.

I think we'll see similar phenomena with the development of the Cancer Center. By eliciting the needs of cancer patients in focus groups, and by support personnel and clinical practitioners coming together to identify the best ways to take care of people, we believe we can creatively put together a comprehensive approach to cancer treatment that will be wonderful.

JM: How do you help people and organizations go beyond even their most positive visions and develop beyond their best values?

MG: I see it as being something that's continually evolving. What's best today is not best tomorrow. If you are committed to a philosophy of quality improvement, then you understand there is no single best. It's all about becoming better. This is about helping people to grow and helping them change their perspective of what they are capable of achieving. It's also about changing the resources and improving competencies.

Medical staff here in Concord really should get the lion's share of the credit on how the organization has evolved. They also should get the credit if we become something different tomorrow. For example, we have cardiac surgeons who allow us to do things we couldn't do before. And those cardiac surgeons wouldn't have been here if there hadn't been first-class interventional cardiologists here before them.

JM: What is the importance and significance of positive thinking in your life—as a human being, a leader, a parent, a partner? What images do you hold?

MG: That's a good question, because I'm not sure that I'm always consistent. I tend to be a person who views the glass as half-full rather than half-empty. I tend to believe that in every challenge there is an opportunity. I believe that people want to succeed. As a human being, I tend to be positive as well. I prefer movies with happy endings to movies with dark endings. I wish sometimes that I maintained the same positive perspective in my personal life that I do in my professional life. Maybe it's because I worry more about my personal life: how my kids will do, etc.

I do think it's really important to try to be positive. I once worked as an assistant administrator and heard that the president of the organization had said something to the effect of, "How could Mike Green be getting anything accomplished when he smiles all the time?" I thought that was somewhat peculiar and it reinforced for me how different my value system was from the culture of that organization. I smile a lot here. It doesn't hurt and it helps to be positive.

JM: Were there appreciative leaders or coaches for you?

MG: I keep hoping that my son, who is an athlete, will have an appreciative coach, because I think it can make all the difference in the world. Very early on in my life, I was fortunate and I had some coaches who pointed out to me that if I ever wanted to be a leader, I needed to use my intensity to pull people rather than push them. It did make a difference.

The Spirit of Inquiry

JM: You teach a class in systems diagrams as part of our Learning Organization leadership program. Participants read Peter Senge's book *The Fifth Discipline* that encourages inquiry. How does inquiry live in you as a leader and in the organization?

MG: Historically, I was pretty conservative, not really anxious to experiment with new and different things. As I've evolved from a leadership standpoint, I've become much more interested in inquiry, because I think that without inquiry you have stagnation. Stagnation is not going to contribute to success, certainly not in today's world. I'm very interested in continuing to try new things and learn from others. I'm also very analytical in that there has to be some rationale as to why it'll contribute positively.

I tend not to be a creative person from a standpoint of the arts. I like music, but can't sing a note. My wife would say that

I'm not very creative. But I think I channel my creative energy into what I do professionally. I always see an opportunity to integrate past experiences and try something different. I also try to learn from others in terms of what their perspectives might be. Even though I'm very analytical, I'm also not afraid to try something on the basis of my intuitive sense. It probably puts me, in some ways, at more risk, but I think you have to have confidence in your intuition, if your intuition is based on the synthesis of a lot of complex information.

JM: "Doing Right Things Right" is a phrase that's used frequently at Concord Hospital, and our employee newsletter celebrates positive actions and events. How do you see us learning from our successes?

MG: We try to do a lot of things here. We do the STAR award (Special Thanks and Recognition), Quality Grams, and try to recognize people doing things right. If people feel gratification, some of it should be intrinsic in terms of gratification you get from doing something right. If you can also put a spotlight on that, they get more inclined to try to do it again. In hockey, that's the thing you really try to capture as a coach. I believe that while winning isn't everything, winning is more fun than losing. If you can teach kids how to win, and they get gratification from winning, then they'll work harder to win again. I think the same thing is true in the workplace. I think if you pose challenges to people, and try to make sure they have the tools to succeed, and they do succeed, then they get a lot of reinforcement.

The Role of Positive Affect in Bringing out the Best

JM: I'd like to explore your experience and your thoughts about the role of hope, inspiration, joy, confidence, or camaraderie, in bringing out the best. Which of these words has a story in your life as a leader?

72

MG: I think the challenge from a leadership standpoint is to be confident without being overconfident or arrogant. I do a fair amount of speaking, whether it's teaching in a small group or speaking to 200 people at a conference. I couldn't get up there and speak if I weren't confident in my ability to communicate in a reasonably intelligent manner.

Confidence is also really important in healthcare today, where you are making decisions that are, in part, based upon your intuition. When we had to re-engineer the workplace, and go ahead with patient-focused work transformation, I had to be confident that essentially what we were doing would work and that we could implement and execute it properly. After all, those were pretty bold initiatives, particularly for an organization that was not used to a lot of change.

Camaraderie, for me, is the enjoyment and respect that I get from my colleagues. I think it's about feeling that we have a shared vision, knowing we can share a laugh, and also knowing we have a lot of hard work to do. It would be very hard to achieve new initiatives, such as Cardiac Surgery, without that sense of camaraderie that helps teams muster the extra energy to face so many challenges.

I think it's very hard to work in a hospital without developing a sense of hope and inspiration. You hear so many sad stories, that if the hope and inspiration of the happy stories do not move you, then you would be lost. And yet, we need to incorporate that hope and inspiration into what we do in support of caring for our patients. Every time I get a letter from a patient who has had an unusually positive experience, it is a source of inspiration for me. It is a source of hope for me like, "Gee, if we did this one time, we ought to be able to do this every time."

JM: I often wonder about people's career journeys and choices they make. What have been the defining moments or choice points in your own leadership journey?

MG: I think the first choice point is always when one decides to be a leader. I don't consider myself to be an extravert, but I chose to learn public speaking in high school because I figured it was essential to becoming a leader. Other decision points for me were placing myself into a line role rather than a professional staff role, and deciding I wanted to be in hospitals.

JM: When did that happen? At Dartmouth? At Sloan School MIT?

MG: If there was a defining moment for me at college, it was when I participated in an Outward Bound program. I was up in the White Mountains of New Hampshire. We were on snowshoes for three weeks, in a cabin for three weeks, and then hiking for another three weeks. I was with three different groups, and it was during that time that I realized I did have capabilities to lead. It helped me recognize that I wanted to be a leader and it also helped with my confidence.

I had wonderful mentors professionally who gave me the opportunity to lead and to make mistakes. I remember in a sophisticated organization, I had put together a proposal to develop a psychiatric unit. I had made a significant error in not consulting with some of the prominent members of the medical staff. If I'd not had that experience, I might not have learned until much later the importance of making sure that you engage others before you lay out great ideas.

JM: How has your leadership philosophy shaped choices that you have made at Concord Hospital?

MG: I guess my leadership philosophy shapes the selection of staff who work with me. I don't want people who are "yes men." I want people who will stand up to me and tell me when I am wrong. So I try to select people who are strong enough to do that. Because of my philosophy and the whole interest I have in inquiry, I try to select people who may be very different from each other. Sometimes, that's where you get the greatest growth and the greatest opportunity to learn. You need to have people who are committed and have high levels of competency. I believe in treating people fairly. I believe in integrity. I wouldn't tolerate having people work for me who are less than open and honest.

My personal philosophy has also shaped me to the extent that, when I have been in the job market, I have not pursued certain opportunities if I felt there was going to be an inconsistency between the philosophy of those organizations and my own personal values. I left an organization once because of such an inconsistency.

JM: As you look back on your leadership career, what advice do you wish you had been given? What would have saved you from bumping into walls?

MG: It's always good advice to tell someone to be patient and I probably could have been more patient on a number of occasions. I wish earlier in my career that somebody had taught me to listen. I'm still not as good at listening as I would like to be. I think that you have to bump into some walls. Maybe there are people who become absolutely unbelievable leaders who never bump into a wall. They may be great leaders, but I'm not sure they're great human beings. I don't know how you can become humble unless you've bumped into walls, and I think humility is a big part of leadership.

JM: What would you tell others about being a leader?

MG: I would tell others that there are a lot of different ways to be a leader. I think being a leader is a combination of education, training, and something internal. But even if you don't have that intrinsic something, you can still lead or contribute to leadership by learning ways around it.

I would also tell anybody that with leadership comes accountability, and if you don't want the accountability, don't be a leader. The leader is ultimately the one that is held accountable when failure occurs. You have to have the self-confidence, that even though you're going to fail—because everybody fails—that you're going to succeed at some point.

I would tell people to understand that leadership can be lonely. If you're the ultimate leader of an organization, I think you have a responsibility to build firewalls of some kind, even between yourself and your closest associates. The toughest decisions may be your decisions. It is only the CEO who is directly accountable to the Board.

I would also share that it is very, very gratifying to be a leader. It's wonderfully gratifying to work with a team that functions well and is successful because of who the people are, and to know that you contribute to it in some small way.

Thomas S. Inui, M.D.

Thomas S. Inui, M.D., President and CEO, Fetzer Institute, Kalamazoo, MI

Penny Williamson

Thomas S. Inui is President and CEO of the Fetzer Institute, a national philanthropic organization devoted to wholeness of mind, body, and spirit in human affairs. A primary care physician, educator, and researcher, he was previously head of general internal medicine, University of Washington School of Medicine, and founding chair of the Department of Ambulatory Care and Prevention, Harvard Medical School.

Dr. Thomas Inui has had a richly diverse career as a physician, a teacher, a researcher, and a leader. He is a person whom many look to for mentorship and wisdom. He combines rare capacities: a formidable intellect; a generous heart and spirit; delight in the unknown; the ability to observe life at multiple levels and to describe accurately and articulately what he thinks, sees, and feels. I can always count on learning something important when I talk with Tom Inui; more than that, I come away feeling enriched as a human being.

Recently, in the fall of 2000, Tom Inui became President and CEO of the Fetzer Institute. As he begins his stewardship of this remarkable organization, Inui talked of actively reflecting on and drawing from his experiences and beliefs as a leader.

Bringing out the Best: Creating Resilient Communities

For Tom Inui, bringing out the best in individuals and groups is tied to the intentional formation of robust learning communities, to which people are drawn both ideologically and by training and expertise, in which there is a mix of a few "old hands," who love the work and are good at it, and a majority of young people with great potential. The group creates high standards of achievement to which each will be held accountable. Tom generates excitement of the unknown where everyone joins, by choice, in an experiment of "together we'll find out if we can do it." Most important, he fosters relationships of trust and openness among all members of the community, where people can learn together through sharing weaknesses and failures as well as successes and strengths.

In Inui's experience, it is work at the deeper human dimension, and particularly around the difficult times, that creates the space for learning. "If you were having a crisis in confidence, you would discover that you were surrounded by people who had also had crises in confidence, and that in their experiences with these problems you would find what you most needed."

In 1986, as leader of the Division of General Internal Medicine at the University of Washington Medical School, Tom was charged with building a program where clinician-teachers could excel in an environment that had traditionally recognized and promoted only clinician-researchers. He assembled a group of faculty who, together, created high standards of success for the unit: clinician-teachers would have to be at the upper-third of all teachers in the Medical School, by evaluations of learners, in order to remain in the department. One faculty member was not able to succeed in this criterion.

Here was a vital faculty member with high ideals and commitment to the work, but who was not measuring up on criteria important to the very existence of the clinician-teacher faculty and, more widely, to the University. The challenge was how to help this person make a successful transition, one in which he felt that leaving the unit and going to do something else was about finding goodness of fit, not about failure.

The transition took about a year and involved all members of the faculty in a thoughtful, caring process that valued and ultimately strengthened both the individual and the group. The senior faculty used their networks to help find an outstanding local practice group that wanted an excellent clinician and part-time teacher. The faculty member received extraordinary emotional support from his peers, and talked openly with them about his strengths and weaknesses, as well as his fundamental desire to take the new job.

The transitioned clinician's openness allowed wider discussions among faculty about the criteria and the struggles that clinician-educators have. They revisited the importance of challenging themselves to succeed across the board, clarified possibilities for getting help when needed, and faced the reality that not everyone would be able to stay. Tom voiced the larger view: "It is essential not to get over-wrought about the importance of any one program. What we do is just part of what medicine does. There is no failure in coming or going; there are lots of ways to find what you most want to do."

Within two years, the individual had joined a practice group that loved him and he loved them, and he was doing the teaching he most liked to do. "It rested upon our ability to surface a very death-dealing issue inside an environment that was supportive for all."

Hearing this story, I was moved by Tom's capacities to hold the well-being of an individual and group with respect, compassion, and clarity; to encourage open and authentic conversations about tough issues among the whole group; to take the time that a situation of this nature called for, in contrast to the leader who acts with brutal swiftness to model "decisiveness"; and ultimately, to transform the essential relatedness of every person involved.

Appreciative Relationships: An Anthropological Leadership Style

Tom Inui's leadership is reminiscent of what an anthropologist colleague referred to as "the original affluent societies"--a phrase used to describe indigenous, subsistence economies where the highest value and most time were given to relationships, and far less was given to the work of meeting daily needs of living. The philosophy was that people are more productive and more creative if time is taken to know each other as human beings. How different from many working relationships where people are "bracketed out," and affluence, time, and productivity are measured quite differently.

As a leader, Inui models "not knowing" and asking for help at every turn. He talked about how important it is to him to hear from people, all people, on a regular basis regarding how he is doing. He also believes that how you ask for feedback is an important determinant of what you get. And so he has a number of avenues: direct requests to peers in age or rank; casual conversations over lunch or after or before work with junior level or support persons who seem willing to speak frankly and openly; and having an administrator who is trustworthy, shows good judgment, and with whom people feel comfortable. Finally, he lets the whole group know that he is interested in a certain issue, would welcome hearing about it directly or through his administrator, and that he will report back on what he's heard. "In that way, people come to trust this set of mechanisms because they hear themselves mirrored back in what I report."

Inui talked about the necessity of taking one's time in a new place, having just taken over the leadership of Fetzer Institute four months before this interview. "It takes careful observation to read a culture accurately: to find key informants, to see who gets work done, who people go to for advice, who knows how things work. It's like a piece of anthropology, and the answers are often surprising." And, like an anthropologist, Inui values and appreciates the stories others have to tell about the culture--willing to not know what is going on and to trust that with time he will be fully and authentically embraced by the community. I was struck by how his approach is so different from the "swashbuckling leadership style" of demonstrating that you have brought salvation from afar and know better, faster, how to "do it."

Later, as I have lunch in the Fetzer Institute dining room, I see Tom in easy conversations with the chefs and wait persons while he is in the food line, and then with various staff members whose table he joins. I watch his relaxed body posture—which conveys attentiveness and a sense of having lots of time—and listen to the laughter that drifts across the room toward me. "Lucky them," I think.

For Inui, the key to building appreciative, authentic, and accepting relationships is to create a safe environment where people can know a good deal about one another, where key senior people love their work and show it, and "where people come to realize that in much of the most difficult work they are radically interdependent with others and that there is no way to solve problems except to collaborate." When senior people model "not knowing," it allows everyone to see that this is the intended way of working, and that "in the crucible of the toughest stuff they do, there is nothing to trust except community and collaboration within it."

In Inui's view, an anthropological approach also serves well in the merger of organizations. Such culturally sensitive leadership was sorely needed in a difficult merger in which Inui was peripherally involved. The merger was between two large Health Maintenance Organizations (HMOs) that came together because of the apparent complementariness of what each had to offer. One was a staff-model HMO known for its high quality and cost effectiveness, but with limited geographic access; the other, a doctor-friendly, preferred provider insurance organization with broad participation by doctors and broad geographic access. The analysis that determined the merger focused on the product lines, processes, and niches in the marketplace. There was insufficient attention to the deep cultures of the two organizations: the one driven by quality and affordability, the other, by growth in the region.

Inside the newly merged entity, it was difficult for the managers to collaborate in deciding how to allocate resources for the future of the organization. Inui's advice was consistent with his prior reflections:

Understand the culture. Take the time to find the people who do the work. Get their perspectives on how and why they're doing what they're doing. The realization that there would likely be major challenges in bringing together these organizations could have led pre-merger discussions about who the leader should be for the coming-together process and what the principle aims and methods of that leader should be. What needs work first in allocating resources that would facilitate that coming together?

Staff Stewardship

Tom Inui wants everyone in an organization, no matter what their function, to feel that their own and others' growth and development is a primary value and concern of the community. It is his goal that there be at least one person, maybe a group, who understands that it is their responsibility to look after, assist, and support the growth and development of each individual. It is only when this is understood that it is possible to approach questions of how to give frank feedback and evaluate performance and, after that, to begin to consider and establish the resources to help people grow through activities such as cross training, educational experiences, sabbaticals, etc. This takes both time and the building of trust so interest is in people, not in forms or procedures.

Positive Image, Positive Action

I asked Tom where and how in organizational life compelling positive images of the future come from. He reflected that, like the Australian Aborigines, we are always capable of being in "Dreamtime" if we can be called back to it. "Dreamtime" is the time of visioning and creating. Sometimes the call can be in the flow of activities, sometimes in retreat.

In a recent search group meeting to fill a key position for a Program Director, Inui began by recalling the group members to their dreams. He said two things: First, that choosing and supporting new people for an organization is the most powerful and important intervention in the history of an organization, as an organization is nothing except the growth and development of individuals in it over time; and second, the particular program that this person would take responsibility for could be seen as a kind of dream they were having about the way they hoped the world could be. He encouraged them to pay attention to their dream as they chose the person, because they had a responsibility for trying to live whatever the dream might be. He then invited people to sit in silence for several minutes and think about what they knew about the program and whom they wanted to have come.

Tom reflected that in retreats, when there is consciously allocated time, it is possible to ask larger questions such as, "What is our calling?" and then to explore and walk around in that question; to ask about particular activities, programs, projects, "What is it about these that represents the dream that we have?" Then it is possible to envision it together and decide what you're going to do as a community. "Of course dreams are unattainable, but that's the beauty of them. Good work is the journey towards them."

Inui is compelling not only because of the words he uses, but also by his pacing and voice tone, all of which convey the emotions, as well as the meanings, he wants to express. When he had finished talking about "Dreamtime," I was reminded of my own deepest dreams by Tom Inui's words and also by his voice. I felt moved by the amazing possibility we have as human beings to be called back at any moment to what most matters to us and by the power of a leader who helps us do so.

Inui reflected that he loves the unattainable, because it's always greater than one imagined it could be. By keeping in mind the long-range vision, as well as local knowledge, and relevant information when making small choices, the result is beyond anyone's capacity to specify, and possibly huge. Inui likened this to when he was practicing as a physician: "I loved the idea that in taking little actions with patients, if I kept all those perspectives in mind, something great, even life-defining, might be happening at every turn."

Being a Durable Optimist

Positive thinking is an integral part of Inui's life. He describes himself as a durable optimist—always expecting good things to happen, disappointed if they don't, but still optimistic. Instead of disaster and catastrophe, he foresaw the possibility of great outcomes from small choices. "We don't know what will happen in these complex and chaotic environments. I choose to believe that I can hold an intent and by the best of my lights make choices that are more likely to move in the direction of good and great outcomes." Like the Navajo, he believes that in some respects, saying something from a particular perspective will make it happen.

If you say to kids, "Oh, you have a funny voice," they are not going to sing. If you say to a faculty member, "Welcome, I hope you can make it. Many haven't and maybe you will," that is so different from saying, "We've chosen you because this part of the world has been waiting for your arrival. And of course this is hard, and we have, of course, chosen for ourselves to specify the conditions of success in such a way as to make it even harder. But success is not up to you alone; this is about us. And when you come to know the truth and robustness of that and trust it in every way, even though you feel it is riskier than anything you have ever done in your life, you will have every opportunity to make this work and when it works...it will be amazing."

It was a thrill to hear those words of belief and challenge spoken on my behalf.

As a doctor, Tom Inui used the placebo effect at every turn: to enhance a patient's self-confidence, to point toward positive outcomes, to strengthen the doctor-patient relationship. He would say with conviction, when he determined what he believed to be the best course of action, "I am so hopeful about this. I bet that a week from now you're going to feel better. And if you don't, I want to be the first person to know, because there are other things to do. But I really think this is going to be good." He clarified, "I use this with faculty. I use it with others. Why? I am a believer and I think it makes a difference to be a believer out loud."

The Spirit of Inquiry

Inui locates "the spirit of inquiry" in his appetite for learning. As a researcher it was what made learning about methods and procedures of research interesting, and the practice of research and emergence of new information compelling. Tom came to understand teaching as "learning with others," and this caused him to shift from lecturing to creating learning-intensive microenvironments. As a manager or administrator, Inui's goal was to create processes of governance and shared resources, as well as institutions to serve the growth and development of faculty. There being no universal recipe for this, Inui collaborated with others in each new community to compose how best to proceed.

He described his preferred learning style: "I like to be immersed in a process with others, then capture and be articulate about the elements of that process that seem most fruitful. Then I like to create a shared work experience of how to proceed. In a specific work environment this can be codified as standards, operating procedures, shared values, and structure of the environment." This is an ecologically driven approach, deriving its power from the particularities of shared history and co-created structures that get disseminated from person to person. If there is a more rapid or wider path for dissemination, Tom Inui hasn't found it.

The Role of Positive Affect in Bringing out the Best: Laughter

Tom commented that hope, inspiration, joy, and camaraderie are all worthy of acknowledgement and celebration, and are important and affective dimensions of life and work. He also spoke of another dimension of work, laughter, as a core part of the basic human condition. Inui spoke of the many faces of humor, for instance, as a detection device. "When something terribly important is being destroyed, as in a pun that destroys language or in 'black humor' that destroys part of our calling, the laughter tells you you've come upon something vital that is at risk." There's the laughter of nervousness, used to dispel tension, laughter to dispel our own pompousness, and laughter just to play, when it's unsafe to do anything else or when it's just fun and silly.

Inui takes laughter seriously and lightly. He spoke of listening in his work groups to the jokes in order to understand the culture and what is really cared about. One day, at a faculty meeting, Inui mentioned that he thought his group had as flat a governance structure (low hierarchy) as any he knew. One of the junior faculty responded, "Well, Tom, it always seems flatter from the top." He realized then that more talk on hierarchy was needed!

Defining Moments in the Leadership Journey: Avoiding Panic Attacks

When Tom figured out, early on, that not knowing things that he thought he should know brought on minor or major panic attacks, and that panic attacks made him "dumb as a stump," he figured out that he could ask for help. This was a defining discovery in his leadership journey, and one that would repeat itself as he took on new and different roles.

As Chief Resident at Johns Hopkins Medical School, Inui described lecturing to his team of physician residents and dreading the moment when he wouldn't know something about a patient or their condition. At first he "froze," and then, "I couldn't remember the name of any drug; couldn't remember what we were supposed to do for the condition. And the more I got wrapped up in the panic, the less I could contribute." His solution was to preempt the whole experience by saying something like: "I think we're going to have to know something about (name the topic, name the question) and I don't know anything about it. Does anybody here? Can anyone here help me?" This led to learning with other people instead of lecturing and, more importantly, it modeled for others that it was acceptable to "not know." Instead of ridicule, there was admiration and progressively more real conversations about what to do. "There were more resources and more resiliency in this community of Hopkins than there had ever been before. It was quite a transition."

Later, as a manager, Inui rediscovered the same approach when facing questions of resource sufficiency. After thinking through all of the possible solutions in one particularly knotty situation—and coming up blank—Tom found himself up at nights in a sweat of trying to solve the issue. He saw it as his job to create the setting in which people could do their best work and grow to their maximum ability. It occurred to him that he was getting "dumber" through lack of sleep and lack of progress—possessed by an unanswerable question. So, he tested out "not knowing" with his administrator and then with the faculty group. The faculty members were pleased to be included in the thinking process and choice of solution, something no one could have arrived at alone as it involved a shared risk by the whole group.

As a clinician, Tom also learned that it was wise to talk openly about mistakes and injuries. He reflected: "I've made mistakes in taking care of people who were dying and going on too long, not attending to what needs to get done before you die. The only salvation has been to talk a lot about it with patients and their families." *Inui recognized that sometimes we try too hard to adapt to unworkable circumstances, before saying, "This isn't what we want, is it?" He has learned the importance of saying that, out loud and early.* Tom talked about being forgiven every time, and growing in his capacity to forgive others, and attributed that to being in caring relationships where learning can happen through mistakes and injuries. "There is very little that I have done alone, by myself. So much of this capacity is relational."

Inui began his leadership journey with the notion that each person has the responsibility to make certain things happen for others. He came to realize that while each leads others in certain ways, the resources and resiliency are in the community and not in any one person. And so, Inui returned to where he began this conversation, re-emphasizing the importance of building environments of trust where people can learn together and risk together in an uncertain world.

Advice and Encouragement

Along the way, individuals have pointed out the inadvisability of Inui's ideas ("quixotic," "too ambitious," "no way to build a career") and then encouraged him to pursue them anyway ("but this is you, go for it!"). Inui has found it helpful to have this kind of paradoxical counsel (clarity about risks mixed with encouragement and support) and tries to do the same for others. He asks whether there is alignment among the motivation of an individual, his ideology, and his work. This is most important because, as Tom concludes:

Work is a bitch. There's so much about it that's hard. If you don't really want to be doing what you're doing, it isn't going to work. So think about it three times. If what you want to do really expresses you and your heart, then let's talk about how it might be possible to make it work.

Dr. Sarah Eagger: The Diamond Approach To Medical Leadership

Dr. Sarah Eagger, Consultant, Old Age Psychiatry, BKCW Mental Health NHS Trust, London, England

Anne Radford

Dr. Sarah Eagger is a Consultant Psychiatrist for the elderly working in a community hospital in London. She is also an honorary senior lecturer at Imperial College School of Medicine. As Chair of the British Holistic Medical Association, she is a much sought-after speaker on integrated medicine, consciousness, and spirituality.

"There are many influences in my work and life—my work with my team, medical students, caregivers, and my medical teaching and spiritual practice. And the image that comes to mind is that of a diamond. Each one of these facets reflects the other. My challenge is to bring these facets together." So began my conversation with Sarah Eagger. And I smiled as I remembered the times I had heard David Cooperrider, a thought leader in Appreciative Inquiry (AI), talk about taking the appreciative approach to organizational change and linking it to the metaphor of Indra's net, where an infinite network of glittering jewels reflect the images of all of the others. Yet Sarah was trained both in Australia and the United Kingdom in the medical model. She works in the public health system in the U.K., the National Health Service, which is under huge pressure to provide good patient care. The pressure is high and most healthcare practitioners find it difficult enough to keep up to date in one model, let alone try to integrate several. So what drives her?

She certainly has a multifaceted life. She is Consultant Psychiatrist for the elderly where she leads a very busy community mental health team for a large, complex area of London. She is an honorary Senior Lecturer at the Imperial College School of

Medicine. She is currently Chair of the British Holistic Medical Association, involved in the Foundation of Integrative Medicine, and is medical advisor to the Janki Foundation for Global Health Care, a charity that supports a holistic hospital in Rajasthan, India. She is on the Steering Committee of the Spirituality and Psychiatry Special Interest Group of the Royal College of Psychiatrists. She also writes and speaks on the subject of spiritual training for people in the caring professions.

And I was curious about the challenge: Why now? What is the message she takes to the consultants she addresses at professional meetings, the multi-professional team she leads, and the students she teaches? What does she have in mind for the caregivers and the patients? Sarah said, "Somehow what I was being taught in medical school didn't quite reflect, for me, the totality of the human condition or deal with all aspects of the patient's pain. I wanted to know something more profound about human nature. How do you really help people; how did you really alleviate suffering?"

Medical training talks about the importance of being empathic, showing compassion, and caring for patients. However, the teaching emphasizes the technical and there is no time to develop skills in the other areas. In their work, practitioners are under increasing pressure to absorb more technical knowledge and to deal with organizational bureaucracy. They often go into a survival mode: giving less of themselves, becoming resentful of the demands patients put on them, and more frustrated with themselves and their colleagues. For many, the gap between what they had hoped for in their careers and what they are living day-to-day is widening.

Sarah's aspiration is to get the balance right between the technical role and the caring role. She believes this balance would be beneficial for both the practitioner and the person receiving the care. This is what she wants to achieve as a leader in her various medical worlds.

The Task of Bringing out the Best in Human Beings and Organizations

From her time as a medical student, Sarah has had questions on how to be with people when they are in pain. These issues are still relevant in her work today as she is in contact with people dealing with loss, traumas, and seemingly incomprehensible, tragic life events. Her search for a "toolkit," some wisdom in this area to help her in her work as a doctor, led her to the British Holistic Medical Association. Their approach attempts to address these issues through a focus on the wounded healer: healing yourself first and understanding the relationship of mind, body, and spirit. The Janki Foundation seminars, with which Sarah has worked, have taken a more spiritually explicit approach in addressing issues such as dying, love, and mental health. There, practitioners are encouraged to mobilize their own values such as respect and higher listening to benefit themselves and their patients.

Bringing out the best in people, for Sarah, is about how she chooses to use her mental energy and how she supports others to use theirs. She is constantly interested in how medical practitioners choose to use their mental energy when they are in a team, working with colleagues, or when they are with patients.

I asked her, when a doctor or practitioner is in a meeting with a patient who is aggressive, how can the practitioner remain calm rather than aggravate the situation? She started talking about mental images such as "cool water to douse the flames" or remaining still and quiet within. Staying observant. Allowing things to emerge when appropriate. Not competing with the other person. At these times, a good leader is working in a very subtle way and not necessarily being seen as the leader. How far, I thought, from the stereotypical image of the medical expert.

These qualities are also important when leading a team. Again, Sarah speaks in images: "If the leader is like a very big tree taking up all the light, there is no room for anyone else to grow." When she first came to her community mental health team, she was aware of some negative energy. However, she also brought her way of thinking--that everyone wanted to feel valued and needed room to grow. As she worked in that way, gradually things changed. The team started coping with the stresses inherent in their work by supporting rather than competing with each other. People started to express their views more openly and to express their appreciation for each other. They began to feel that leadership resides in the team rather than in one person.

Continuing with the nature metaphor, Sarah believes the community mental health team still needs tending. People can feel beleaguered because of the stresses in the work and their morale can drop. This is the time when appreciative leadership needs to be even more subtle. "Less is more...and it is what you do in the 'less' that is important," Sarah says. "This is the time when your choice of energy is really important. It needs to be the energy that will facilitate, enhance, or enable whatever is going on in the room whether it is with a patient or the team." This energy can show in little ways such as with humor, bringing out the funny side of people even in tragic situations. It can also show when telling people they are doing a good job in a situation, where it would be very easy to be critical.

Sarah was tested several times on her style of leadership when she arrived to lead the team.

One person, in particular, believed I had done something I hadn't and was very angry with me. I needed to stay calm and stay with my belief in myself. I needed to listen to her view of me without giving in to her negativity by retaliating or denying what she had to say. I was then able to say to her directly and calmly, "I didn't see myself in that way." Gradually, over the years, the person's attitude changed. My approach was to indicate that I was going to work with her despite her dislike for me, and that I was going to be consistent with her.

The time when Sarah became most aware that the team really appreciated her and that their attitude toward her had changed was when she got married. "They held a lovely lunch for me. They all came and several even made speeches. It was a very moving occasion."

As the leader of the community mental health team, Sarah also needs to give feedback to the junior doctors during the short time they are with the team. This is potentially a very difficult situation; it can be critical, negative, and demoralizing for the junior doctor and an ego trip for the person in charge. Sarah takes a different approach. She wants to give inspirational feedback, setting out what she wants the junior doctor to aspire to in his/her practice, in terms of working with others. At the end of a feedback session, the junior doctors would know what they needed to change and be clear about the goals they wanted to achieve. She is also aware that, as a role model, she needs to demonstrate the qualities of an effective doctor; namely, to be compassionate, to show humility, as well as to be honest and constructive.

Appreciative Relationships

The previous examples indicate the value and role of appreciation in fostering close working relationships. In another example, Sarah talked about how showing her own vulnerability helped in a breakthrough with another colleague. There had been a strain in the relationship that led to a confrontation. At one point she said, "I'm sorry, I'm under an enormous amount of stress here and I'm struggling to keep lots of different things together. I was trying to communicate efficiently with you, and I'm sorry if I came across as terse." From then on, the communication improved since the other person had been misinterpreting her body language. Sarah learned that she must give time for the relationship. She became aware that situations were resolved in a much better way when she put the relationship in the middle of the situation rather than the task. "Putting the task first may get the job done, but you lose so much, it's not worth it."

Authentic, appreciative, and accepting is what the good leader of a medical team needs to be every second of the day. Being that role model and choosing to use the mental energy to bring together the necessary technical, emotional, and spiritual knowledge is a constant challenge and a constant learning. For people like Sarah and her medical colleagues, the next level of learning is about drawing on their deeper resources to provide an even more valuable level of care. What would happen if, by connecting to a higher source, they could use their mental energy to create a spiritual antidote and use that, in addition to the medical remedy?

According to Sarah, "Appreciative relationships in this team are also about being with each other—taking some time to know each other as people, knowing what is going on in each others' lives, and having some social time together. It is also about giving people the space to talk about personal things like values when they are ready to do so." Some people in the team were surprised to know of Sarah's interest in spirituality. Yet, by expressing her views quietly, as she does, others were encouraged to say what was important for them. One day, this awareness was very helpful.

> I walked into the ward and the situation was chaotic: fewer staff than usual, some patients were very agitated, and staff felt overwhelmed. I had to deal with four or five things very quickly. After that, everyone came back into the room and I said, "I think we need a few moments of silence to calm down so that we can continue. Meditate, pray, reflect—do whatever you need to do to calm down." Everyone joined in! And it was very powerful. And I felt I was really being authentic; I needed to get some energy from a higher source.

Being authentic in the moment worked for everyone.

Positive Image and Positive Action

If people in a team feel contained, supported, and respected by others, they are able to be creative and feel they have the space to come up with all sorts of suggestions. This is the situation with Sarah's team at this time. It means that in meetings where some new thinking is needed, people feel playful and relaxed about bringing up many different ideas without fear of being judged or criticized. People can then get into lateral thinking and building on each other's ideas so that truly innovative suggestions emerge.

I was curious about playfulness. How had the group arrived at that point? Can any group be playful? Sarah responded, "Putting plenty of energy into relationships was important. Having a shared passion was also important—in this team it was about patient care. And that said volumes about the values shared in the group; they knew what was important to the whole group by being there."

The importance of building relationships and loving generously is emphasized as is cultivating good humor, allowing people their contradictions, living love, and looking out for the positive. Sarah recalled that, in a recent meeting:

A colleague came out with some off-the-wall comments, and everyone laughed. And yet, his thinking expanded our horizons and we went on to develop something new. He is usually the one who says the "unsayable." Then, we go beyond our thought patterns into a new place and spontaneously create something together.

The Spirit of Inquiry

There is a tendency in the public health system to keep things as they are. Staff come and go, so it can be reassuring to keep the systems fixed. Another way that Sarah has helped to keep the team "light" is to say that systems can be changed. She encourages people to look into different ways of doing things. "To encourage the spirit of inquiry, you have to have a front door to your organization that welcomes people and encourages them to act on their own inspirations."

And what supports this? Sarah explained that it is "a willingness to change and take on new ways of getting the job done. An ability to trust that the person will use their energies creatively where they see they are needed." Sarah recognized that the way of working when she first joined the team: "Don't change anything around here, don't give me anything more to do," is counterproductive to delivering the kind of care the team wants to deliver.

By creating a good atmosphere of cooperation and relationship, there are opportunities to discuss issues, such as strategy, and to set an example by volunteering to take something forward. People then see that energy and respond to it. They can see that cooperation pays off.

The Role of Positive Affect in Bringing Out the Best

Sarah spoke about the importance of sharing:
Sharing in each other's joy and each other's grief has brought our team very close. There was an awful situation where the very young son of a team member died. And the team was able to respond. With the kind of work we do, there are tragedies and wonderful stories. Sharing both has been important for the team. It means we are whole people

and we are being authentic with each other.

For me, there is a direct link between having the capacity to care for the people you work with and the quality of care you can give to your patients. If you are feeling supported by your team, you will provide quality care. If you feel at odds with them or the organization, you will not. This link is the most powerful model for providing good patient care.

It appears that some of the defining moments for a professional can be in those special moments with patients. Sarah talked about one such patient.

He had looked after his wife for many years and became depressed when she died. He was so low I suggested he come into the hospital, but he didn't like it. He left after two days. He went home without going through the formal discharge procedures and locked himself indoors without the medication or any of the support I had been trying to arrange for him. Several weeks later, he came to outpatient services and was concerned that I might have been annoyed with him. I said that I had been worried for him and that he needed to remember that. He said he was only human. I said, "Don't forget, I'm only human, too." We looked at each other and laughed. Since then, we have had a good relationship and he continues to make progress. This is when all the other agencies had given up on him.

And this reaffirms my belief that I give good patient care when I relate to the patient as an individual, showing that I am a human being who worries and thinks about them. It is about being direct and clear while showing care and compassion. It is about bringing all those facets together.

As our interview came to an end, I smiled again. What a wonderful opportunity I had just had to find out more about a person who is quiet, unassuming, and who was surprised to be asked to take part in this study. She manifestly lives the life of an appreciative leader. She is like an individual Indra's net where everything in her reflects and is connected to everything else.

Chapter Four

Serving The Community

Three community leaders—a police chief, a school superintendent, and a director of a technical/vocational education department—speak about their philosophies, challenges, and satisfactions. Chief Peter Carnes, now heading the police department in a Cape Cod town, discusses the undergirding of his far-reaching collaborative, community-building ways. Annette Griffin, 2000-2001 Superintendent of the Year in Texas, reflects on the values that have contributed to her ability to turn around cultures by honoring individual, system, and community needs. Kathi Mullin, an administrator in the Boston Public School System, uses "clarity of purpose" and the guiding force of her mother, to sustain the courage of her many convictions.

Appreciative Leader, Architect
Of An Appreciative System

Chief of Police Peter L. Carnes, Yarmouth Police
Department, Yarmouth, Massachusetts

Gerald T. Gallagher

*Chief Carnes began his police career at age 18 in Wenham, MA
and was named chief there at age 31. He is past President of the
Massachusetts Chiefs of Police Association. An adjunct faculty
member, he holds a BS in Law Enforcement and an MS in Criminal
Justice.*

Do you remember your last meeting with your local police
officer? Was it an appreciative experience? In Yarmouth,
Massachusetts on Cape Cod, there have been some major changes
in the police department led by Chief Peter L. Carnes. The "new"
Yarmouth Police Department, I propose, is the result of an
appreciative leader forming an appreciative system. "Leadership
can never stop at words. Leaders must act, and they do so only in
the context of their beliefs. Without action or principles, no one
can become a leader," Max DePree wrote in *Leadership Jazz*.

The chief's description of his leadership principles and beliefs
is impressive. The whole system change that has resulted from this
leadership is exciting, particularly occurring, as it did, in a para-
militaristic, police department culture.

Bringing out the Best in Human Beings and Organizations

"This department was a rich oil well under the ground and,
prior to Chief Carnes's arrival, the oil trickled slowly into the
community. After he arrived, he tapped the full potential in the
organization. The flow into the community dramatically increased,
as he controlled it by opening and closing the valve as needed."
Deputy Chief Michael Almonte used this metaphor when asked to
explain the changes brought to the Yarmouth Police Department
(YPD) since the arrival of Chief Peter Carnes.

The improvements are impressive: a new $7 million plus headquarters building; new higher rankings in the department; and newly initiated programs such as "Citizen Police Academy," "Adopt-a-School," "Project UnGun," and "Cop Cards," are all examples of the extrinsic measures Peter Carnes brought to Yarmouth. The chief, members of his department, and the town administration described these improvements to me with great pride and passion. Equally impressive are the regard the community has for, and the pride the officers have in, the police department. Most impressive is the respect and admiration the police officers confer on Carnes. "My greatest fear," said one officer, "is that he leaves us to go to another job."

Town Administrator, Bob Lawton, described the videos that the finalists for the chief's position were asked to prepare back in 1995. One video was of Carnes's competitor speaking at Town Meeting, asking the voters to approve a rather large expenditure for the police department. The second video depicted Carnes speaking to the press after a shooting in town. Lawton told me that Chief Carnes was certainly positive, forceful, and impressive as he addressed the "audience." What differentiated him from the other applicant was how positively he spoke of his people, his police officers, and the job that they had done for the department and in the investigation of the shooting. He began speaking well of his people before he got the job, and he definitely didn't stop when he got the job.

"The only time I saw the chief angry--and you can tell by the expression and color of his face--was the time an officer criticized another officer in his presence. We found out quickly that was something he didn't like and that we shouldn't do," said Sgt. Rob Warren. He does deal with the negative, but that is not his focus, both Officer Mike Almonte and Administrator Lawton reported. The letters that he sends to Town Hall are about the good, not the negative. "I can't go around giving $10 bills to everyone, but I can show my appreciation through my letters to the town officials," says the chief.

The appreciation of Peter Carnes for his officers comes in many packages. An officer told me, after the chief had been in the department only two years, that he spoke for over five minutes—without notes—at an awards ceremony, describing the officer's career highlights. "He said things I had forgotten."

Shared leadership is another of the innovations introduced by the chief. An officer, who has a particular skill or interest in one of the activities of the department, is encouraged to participate and, at times, to lead an activity. These activities have included firearm teams, uniform committees, mountain bike patrol, adopted schools, and many others. "I've been blown away by the job some guys have done. I didn't know it was in them," said one officer. "It used to be that there was an 'A' team and a 'B' team and one got all the jobs and the other got none. Now everyone has an opportunity to show what they can do," related another. "We did not know what we could do until Chief Carnes gave us the chance." The chief affords them the freedom to experiment, which also implies that failure is possible. One of the officers said, "We are so proud of our department, our fellow officers, and the trust that the chief has shown in us that we work extra hard so we don't fail."

The appreciative leader provides the opportunity for his or her people to demonstrate and take pride in individual achievement. The organization then benefits by utilizing all the varied talents of its people. "When I came here, there were a number of officers of retirement age who stated that they didn't need the hassle of breaking in another chief as they would soon be gone. They're still here," according to Carnes. Appreciative leaders create appreciative employees.

Appreciative Relationships

"All police departments depend on camaraderie. We are a family and we have to be. We can't be out there alone because the odds are against us. We cry together; we laugh together. This department is like others in that respect, but where we are different is that we have taken our leader, our chief, into our family. He is one of us. In other places the chief is like a god, up on a pedestal, someone to respect, but also someone to stay away from."

Officer Mike Bryant went on to say, "We don't lose people to other departments, they come to us. Of the last ten or so people hired, about half came from other police forces. One sergeant came to us to be a patrolman; the only officer we lost to another department went to the state police, which is much larger than us and has more opportunities."

Chief Carnes was invited into the camaraderie of officers. He is not "up there," someone to be avoided, or distant, but he is available, approachable, and signals that he will listen. Is this any surprise given that one of the chief's first actions upon arriving in Yarmouth was to have a private, hour-long meeting with each of the 60-plus members of the department? He asked them questions about themselves and the department. For many of those people it was the first time they had ever been in the chief's office and the first time they had been asked what they wanted or how they felt.

Authentic relationships produce authentic feedback. Officer Bryant is the President of the YPD local of the International Brotherhood of Police Officers. "I get to battle with the chief," he said with more than a hint of a smile on his face. Turning serious he said:

We agree to disagree. If we disagree, we bring the matter up to the next level as the contract dictates. No matter the outcome, the chief does not hold a grudge; he does not take it personally. The officers know that they can step up and complain; they will be heard and it won't be held against them. He and I meet once a week to discuss things before they become problems. That way there are no surprises; the officers know where he's coming from.

Similarly, Police Chief Carnes says there has to be a bond between management and labor. "Communication must be maintained both ways and you have to have faith in your people and don't give up on them." The appreciative leader listens to his union, has an understanding that conflict can occur, and deals with it under predetermined guidelines with no repercussions.

The chief speaks of the similarities between the police and the clergy. "We both have high standards of conduct in the community. We see it all, but sometimes we can't tell all." On too many occasions, he has stood on a doorstep, usually with clergy, bringing the news of a loved one's unexpected, tragic death to a family. The

101

relationship and bonding with the clergy is very important to the chief and not only in times of tragedy. He credits the police chaplain in Wenham with helping him shape a portion of his personal philosophy. "I tie the church into what I do. I think there's more to what we are doing, I think someone is calling the shots."

Positive Image and Positive Action

"Police departments have a tremendous amount of power," states the chief. "Under certain circumstances, we can take away your freedom, we can take away your life. Because of this, we can never give enough training." Prior to Carnes's arrival, the department assigned a police officer in the high school. The chief believed that the high school years were too late as the kids had already formed strong behavior patterns. They had to be taught earlier. For example, they had to know how and why to wear a seat belt when they were still in grade school. In the "Adopt a School" program, an officer volunteers and then is assigned to a school in town. Now, it is not uncommon to see a police cruiser at a grade school or to see a uniformed officer talking to a third-grader. This used to be a sign of trouble. Now the officers' presence is a normal occurrence as they arrive to do more training or just be visible in a positive way.

As might be expected, a number of positive situations developed from these new "cop-kid" relationships—initiated from both directions. A senior officer told me that one of the officers in the program had asked for more radar patrols on a certain street that was notorious for speeding cars. Why the new request? "That's my school on that street—those are my kids," was the answer. The officer didn't wait for orders from on high to address a problem he considered his own. In another example, several officers were called to the high school to quell a disturbance. An officer said that when they arrived it appeared to be a near-riot type situation. "I approached one of the leaders of the group. It was a very tense situation with a number of the guys looking to back him up. And I will never forget this female student coming around the corner, looking at me, and saying, 'That's Officer Y; he's a good guy.' " End of disturbance.

Carnes, as the affirmative leader, has brought new and dynamic change to the department and the community by providing the opportunity for positive interaction. The affirmative interaction feeds on itself and grows. "An officer in one of the schools asked if he could have several hundred YPD cards because he wanted to send one to each of his kids on their birthday, signed Officer Rob."

When I asked the chief for the sources of the positive images of the future, he said:

From our people. We are all stakeholders. We are all team players. During a citizen's meeting, a man asked me where we got officer "x." He had just made a great presentation and really impressed the audience. I told him that he had been on the force for 20 years and now he was getting out into the community to show what he could do.

The chief calls this "visibility of ability."

An officer told me that the trust Peter Carnes has in him means more to him than any pay raise or any written commendation. The chief's attitude is: "This is the problem, these are the facts, you make the decision." The chief's attitude was more strongly stated by one of his officers, "He truly likes being a cop. This is like his hobby." Another told me, "He is the ultimate professional; he is self-confident, and he is not intimidated by the success of others." A more positive image, for a department leader, is difficult for me to imagine.

The Spirit of Inquiry

Comments expressed by YPD officers suggest that inquiry happens when it needs to happen and not on some predetermined schedule. Inquiry is serious listening.

He could have four people in his office, a couple waiting, two phones going at once, and when he sees an officer wanting to see him he'll come right out and ask, "What do you need?" When you are talking to him nothing else is going on. You are the most important person in his life at that time. He is not looking over your shoulder to find someone more important to talk to.

In keeping with the chief's view that everyone is a stakeholder, Carnes reported this story, "At the town dump, of all places, this man approached me and said he was against the new police headquarters building. I asked why and he said it was going to be too expensive if we had to buy private land. You should build it on public land." Based on that conversation, a search for available, town-owned land began. Some excess school property was found, and nearly a million dollars was saved. The building is now under construction after being approved by ballot vote by the citizens. Not only was the chief approachable at the town dump, he also initiated dialogue. He asked the extra question, he discovered the emotions behind the statement, and he took it seriously enough that he changed his course of action.

Inquiry became a major reality in Yarmouth when the chief started the Citizen Police Academy. The chief wanted the people to have a working knowledge of his department and his officers to know the people they were serving. In Yarmouth, the Citizen Police Academy is a major commitment—the meetings are three and one half hours each night for 11 weeks as well as a Saturday session. More than 200 diverse Yarmouth citizens have graduated. "They come in here the first night, most of them very nervous," Lt. Steven Xiarhos told me. "But then the chief and I joke about our hair—the chief is, should we say, challenged in that area—and they laugh and become more at home in our home. They learn what we do and why we do it. I've seen some of the most hardened officers giving a high five after spending four hours with a citizen in their patrol car." The officer and citizen have shared an appreciative experience.

The Role of Positive Affect in Bringing out the Best
Peter Carnes's father, a part-time policeman and volunteer fireman in Wenham, Massachusetts, was his inspiration to become a police officer and his first mentor. From his father, who was actively involved in the Wenham community, he developed his interest in community service and chose this direction for his career. He eventually served on the Wenham police force. All of his mentors in Wenham—his chief, the vice president of the hospital, the department chaplain, and his father—all served the community

on nights and weekends, whenever there was a need. These lessons are still with him as he leads his police force. "We are the only social agency open 24 hours a day and seven days a week," is the chief's way of putting it. The chief describes Wenham as a small town where knowing most all the citizens forced the police to be a part of the community; neither group was able to be anonymous. These experiences formed the basis for his emphasis on "community policing," the partnership of the police and the community, which he brought to Yarmouth.

Carnes's effect on his department has been far-reaching and deeply impacting. An officer described two visits to the department by retired officers who had not worked for the chief. One said, "I wish I could work for this chief." The other was crying as she left. "I'm okay. I'm crying because I am so happy for you guys." "He could leave, but we would be all right," declares Officer Steven Xiarhos. "He's taught us how to do it." These testimonials reminded me of what Walter Lippman stated in the *New York Herald and Tribune* in April 1945, after the death of President Franklin Roosevelt: "The final test of a leader is that he leaves behind him in other men the conviction and the will to carry on."

"Chief Carnes live and breathes community policing," quotes Mike Almonte. The spirit of community policing is also found in their Mission Statement which states in part: "We the members of the Yarmouth Police Department, believe that a joint effort with an empowered community will allow us to make decisions reflecting the cultural diversity of the community with respect for the dignity and rights of all individuals." The statement ends with, "We pledge to innovatively solve problems with the community providing our citizens with an improved quality of life."

A story, related to me by one of the officers, is an example of how the citizens are being ensnared in this appreciative system net. "A citizen came into my office and proceeded to tell me how well and how thoroughly two officers had conducted an investigation of a small property loss on his property. He continued on for some time describing all that the officers had done, and then a bit teary eyed, he said he wanted to donate one of his paintings for our new building. I knew it was valued in the thousands."

In another story I was told, a selectman approached the town administrator and reported that his wife had been stopped for speeding. "Oh, no, another thing I'll have to deal with," thought the manager. Instead the selectman finished the story by saying the officer had pointed out the dangerous curve up ahead and that major accidents had occurred there. His wife wanted to express her gratitude for the manner in which she was treated. "We are often hearing good things about our police department," said the administrator.

Yarmouth is bounded by water on two sides, Cape Cod Bay on the north and Nantucket Sound on the south. Appropriately, Officer Mike Almonte, who I call the department "metaphorist," chose a nautical metaphor to describe Carnes's Yarmouth Police Department, "The chief just started the wave. The waves increased as more officers helped him improve the department, so that eventually even those who weren't out there making waves were carried along by the momentum, and then we all began to surf together."

Positive Thinking *In Action*:
Appreciative Leadership

Kathleen A. Mullin, Director of the School-to-Career Programs, Boston Public Schools, Boston, Massachusetts

Joan M. Vitello

Kathleen Mullin has been the Director of Boston school system's largest reform efforts of the 1990s, the School-to-Career initiative. Most recently, she orchestrated the strategic plan to restructure the system's technical/vocational education. Among other awards and professional recognition, she received the Henry L. Shattuck Award for Outstanding Public Service in 1992.

Introduction

I have known Kathleen "Kathi" Mullin my entire life. We grew up together in Boston, played together, and, for more than 48 years, supported each other in the joys, sorrows, and concerns of life. I have always been proud of her accomplishments and, recently, I was able to directly witness Kathi in her role as Director of School-to-Career Technical/Vocational Programs for the Boston Public Schools, where she has worked for twenty-six years, beginning as a classroom teacher. Over the years, I had heard of the extraordinary leadership and the high recognition accorded her, which includes being the recipient of the Henry L. Shattuck Award for Outstanding Public Service, the highest public service award in Boston. During my tenure as a consultant, I was finally able to experience firsthand the healthy culture that she created, the productive staff that she brought together, and the ethos of caring and commitment that permeated the School-to-Career Programs and, indeed, the Boston Public School community.

I was struck by her direct, positive manner. "No negative talk. We have too much work to do. For the serious and important work to get done, we cannot afford to waste time no matter how natural at times these behaviors might be. Leave your ego at the door," states this attractive, perky woman. Kathi does not tolerate negative conversation in the office. She models her intolerance by acting positively, often in the face of adverse times. For Director Mullin, there is always a positive side to situations, always an alternative. She's the ultimate problem solver and positive thinker. She blends realism with optimism so that the morale remains high among her staff and the "serious work gets done." In fact, her optimism is contagious and her humor is infectious. Kathi's role modeling has facilitated a positive, productive work environment at the School-to-Career Office where she has been the director for over eight years.

How does she demonstrate positive thinking *in action*? I sought to find out in conversations with Kathi and those who worked with her.

The Task of Bringing out the Best in Human Beings and Organizations

Kathi Mullin brings out the best in people and in the organization by modeling a positive approach and showing others that "negative talk" is unacceptable. She gives immediate, open, and often humorous reminders that she and her staff are here for the children, that they must remember the mission, which she has instilled in the department. That mission is to ameliorate the effects of poverty and oppression and improve the quality of education for children to reach their fullest potential. Kathi further responded, "I really want kids to be able to make the connections between what they learn in the classroom and the real world, and to make it relevant....In order to do that, I have to be strategic in planning who is going to come into this organization and be able to work as a team member. Every one of us has an ego, but I had to really model, early on as a leader, that you leave that [ego] at the door."

Another colleague commented that Kathleen has created "an ethos of caring and commitment." When I asked Kathi about this observation, she responded, "I'm a person of strong conviction. I truly believe that if you can build environments where young people are really engaged, motivated to learn, and have caring adults in their lives, you can make a difference. That's what I'm about."

Kathi's department has become a place where many staff members have learned, through her example, to recognize the strengths that each of them has, to fulfill the job each has accepted, and to leave no room for negative talk. Mullin's staff often laughs in response to the positive quips that she uses to quickly nip any negative behaviors. The power of her organization lies with the laughter. The staff members in Kathi's department have become more serious, more dedicated, more involved, and more empowered about the critical nature of the work that remains to be done in order for the mission to be realized.

As director, Kathi has not only allowed the empowerment to happen, she continuously embraces it. I asked Kathi about whether the empowerment of her staff could be a scary thing for a leader. "Absolutely not," was her reply and she smiled confidently as she said this. The refreshing absence of insecurity in this leader brings with it the feeling that she trusts and respects her staff members, and expects the same in return. It was no surprise that Kathi said that, "Trust and respect are my two most solid values."

Kathi tells a story that was truly a high point for her, and a high point for students with disabilities. It launched a new way of thinking and changed a system that was not necessarily serving students in preparing them for their post-high school life. The story is about the time when Kathi believed that a student with disabilities needed to learn how to use the public transit system and to stop using the home school bus. Then when high school ended, he would know how to get around on his own, use the community, get a job, make friends, go places, and live outside of the walls of his home.

The acting superintendent was more than hesitant about the idea of "travel training" or removing the door-to-door transportation made available by the school system. Issues of liability took priority over the quality of life of this student and his development. Kathi remembers meeting with the acting superintendent and digging down deep into both her belief system of what kids need and her desire not to give up. She said to him, "Isn't this what we are here for? It's more of a liability to allow this young man to leave this school system and never be able to access his own community because we did not teach him how." Kathi's face got a bit red as she recalled this experience.

This was a big turning point; I had the guts to do this. I looked at these young people and I found out they were going nowhere except school. No friends, no movies, no jobs. Nothing. Nowhere. They were locked up in their homes. So I went out and started job programs for kids with disabilities. I travel trained them myself. They had to get around on public transportation or they would never go anywhere after high school ended. I'd get up at 6:00 in the morning and have little index cards with me. I'd show the students the cards with pictures on them of the different stops and landmarks and tell them with the pictures where we get off, at what stops. I did a lot of that. I saw this former student about a year later at the Back Bay train station and he was getting a newspaper. I said, "Chris? Who's the newspaper for?" since I knew that Chris didn't read. And he said, "Kathi, I bring it to work," and I said, "That's great," and he said, "Everybody at work reads a newspaper at break time so I'm reading one, too!" I said, "This is great!" I was so excited because he was buying a newspaper like everyone else, and taking the train, and working. This was the same young man! And I said to myself, "God, I feel good!" So, that's what it's all about.

That is one example of Kathi bringing the best out in people. She brought the best out in the students, that's clear, but she also brought the best out in the acting superintendent and others who, realizing the potential of these students, came around to institute the idea of travel training and to create job programs for students with disabilities. She brought the best out in herself, too, because she didn't give up. She remained professional and rational and took all the steps she needed to take to make sure this student and others like him would find their way in life.

I asked Kathi who she remembered really appreciating *her* and how she knew that they did. She quickly responded that past teachers and students and current staff members have shown appreciation. They make statements directly to her and have sent notes of gratitude. There have been tokens of appreciation that people have sent her, ranging from baskets of flowers to formal plaques of appreciation and even to humorous figurines. But Kathi added something far more telling of the kind of leader and human being that she is. She said that she feels truly appreciated by knowing that the work in her department is getting done around her and that she can rest at night knowing that. This is her concept of appreciation. To me, it's another reminder of the highly moral person Kathi Mullin is.

Appreciative Relationships

I felt that since I knew Kathi so well, I might put too much of my own ideas into her stories. So I sought out others to help me. One of her staff members offered the following: "Forget all the negative things that might go on in a job. Look at this person who we work for. Look how great this environment is because of Kathi. Look at what she did for technical vocational education, which was really in trouble. Kathi did what she had to do and still with respect for the people it affected."

One of the strategies that Kathi uses to develop a feedback rich environment at work and to help her staff to appreciate each other happens when she leads staff meetings. She begins by offering everyone a chance to say something positive or to recognize some act about someone else.

Kathi said she believes strongly in enabling her employees to feel good about themselves and to have ownership in their work. This certainly allows them to be feeling psychologically empowered to do the best work possible. Kathi stated, "I knew early on that if I was to work with this really diverse group, I had to look at each one individually and figure out what makes them tick. I had to draw from their strengths, not look at their weaknesses."

Kathi's advice is to always remain patient and to have trust. I probed a bit deeper about patience. She added,

It's easy to forget to be patient with different people, all with different personalities, but you need to. You need to listen. You need to trust that they might have a contribution to make and that will help to keep the cooperation going.

It's easy to get antsy, but I try always to be patient. As a leader, you need to stop thinking about yourself and concentrate on others' needs. It's hard, but it can be done.

Positive Image and Positive Action

Asking Kathi questions about facilitating positive images and positive actions was like asking fish about water. I felt almost silly asking these questions since positive thinking is so natural for Kathi, part of her life, and part of the way she directs and guides her staff to evoke positive images. She began by saying that an important part of her daily life is remembering the Serenity Prayer: "God grant me the Serenity to accept the things I cannot change, the Courage to change the things I can, and the Wisdom to know the difference."

Kathi believes strongly in bringing outside counselors and facilitators into the department. They bring objective views about ways to improve group dynamics and to facilitate positive visions among the group. This way she can be more a part of the group, not strictly the leader or director. The outside facilitation has given the staff the luxury of reflecting about their work, their relationships with each other, how things could be improved and which things were working amazingly well. Kathi helps people go beyond their current visions and ideas. She offers time to reflect. She takes all ideas seriously and helps staff members in the organization move ideas into action.

As a leader, as a parent, as a partner, Kathi Mullin continues to keep what seems to have become a mantra in her thoughts: to have respect and trust for others. In her own life, through joyful moments and times of celebration, as well as during times of conflict, loss, and struggle, she says, "Stay positive; positive thinking is both natural and a requirement."

The Spirit of Inquiry

Mullin always questions the intent and purposes of innovations and ideas. But she then quickly added the following comment: "Bringing out the best in people in an organization means that you must let them run with the innovations they come up with and allow them to present their projects." Kathi looked serious, "My advice to others would be, 'Don't rape your employees of their ideas.'" She tries to "mentor and build employees, not tear people down." She continues,

It can be tiring and I do get angry sometimes, but by allowing my employees to work on their goals or ideas, they help me meet my own goals. Together we work on goals and together we inquire into and question what we are doing. We always ask the following: "Is it student-centered?" Anything we do must affect children in positive ways....I am really serious about combating poverty. It must be combated. It affects everything. I think when we allow our employees to run with good ideas that are good for children, we might ultimately fight poverty in the end.

I asked her to address the idea of "catching people doing something right," as Ken Blanchard, the organizational development expert, suggests. Kathi often walks around the department greeting people, thanking them for the work they are doing. When she recognizes that her employees have been working hard or have created something significant, she celebrates it by making formal announcements of the accomplishment. Kathi tries to encourage positive work by drawing on her staff's strengths, finding out what each person is good at, and working with those strengths.

The Role of Positive Affect in Bringing out the Best

Kathi talked about the defining moment in her journey as a leader. She said it happened, not too long ago, after she had been a leader for quite some time. She made the decision to stay in the school system after she received a very attractive offer to leave for a higher position in another school district. She explained that this was her defining moment because she realized that despite the many advantages of the other employment offer, she wanted, "down deep," to remain in Boston, and to keep working toward fulfilling the mission. In making this decision, she explained: "It helped me to come full circle. Once I made the decision to stay, I got re-energized and I then re-energized my staff."

Mullin's job is fast paced and she reminded me that she oversees 49 individuals. At times decisions must be made quickly but she tries to make them with her moral compass in hand by saying, "You must respect people, let them maintain their integrity, while recognizing your inner feelings and, at the same time, not losing sight of the goal."

Interviewing Kathi has been as inspiring as having known her for these 48 years, for I am her older sister, and up until now our career paths have never intermingled. Kathi is not only my sister, but also my friend and now a role model for the kind of leader I strive to be. She exemplifies an appreciative leader and an honest human being with a truly good and moral soul and an obvious sense of purpose.

In addressing the topic area of "positive affect in bringing out the best," I felt it was necessary to describe some of the inspiration that she offers as a leader and to discuss aspects of her personal life that I believe might have led to her becoming an appreciative leader. I asked her Program Developer, Sandy Copman, to share some of her prior experiences with Kathi. She states,

> By way of background, Kathi and I first worked together to facilitate job training and recreational programs for Boston youth with disabilities, young adults whose disabilities were compounded by the fact that they were poor. Some had terminal illnesses. Most had been isolated from the community except for attending public school. We worked together to decrease the isolation and create ways for these students to enjoy the many aspects of community life. We were successful, I am proud to say, and since those days, I have grown to understand, know, and respect Kathi even more, and to learn from her wisdom, her optimism, and her life experiences.

Kathi has a toughness and a tenacity to beat all odds, and an appreciation of the love and the good in people. Kathi goes about the daily job of striving towards meeting goals regardless of potential obstacles. The glass is always half full and, if one way doesn't work, she'll think of another strategy. She rarely gives up trying to meet goals and overcome obstacles, and she certainly does not give up hope. Kathi is rugged enough to bear the often difficult dynamics of working in a large public city school system, yet she is not an intimidating leader. Rather, she is revered and respected by many colleagues, parents, and students.

From talking with and knowing Kathi, it is clear that our mother's rearing practices and unconditional love had a great deal to do with the roots of this extraordinary leader and highly moral human being. Our mother always showed total care and concern for her children—first and foremost—and reminded us of her love always, offered us constant verbal rewards for doing good, for being strong in the face of dire times and, like Kathi, for celebrating the good times and the good people. Thank you, Ma, and thank you, Kathi.

The Power Of Love: Appreciative Leadership

Annette Griffin, Superintendent, Carrollton-Farmers Branch Independent School District, Dallas, Texas

Nancy Oelklaus

An educator since 1970, Annette T. Griffin is known as an appreciative leader who builds and strengthens parental and community support for schools and students. A graduate of Louisiana State University and the University of North Texas, Griffin has also studied at Harvard and Columbia Universities.

> What I see is not what I'm looking at, but what I'm looking with. And so my first and principal duty... is to find my eyes of love.
>
> Dan Jones

In the Silicon Hills of Texas, technology companies build the brains of computers called silicon chips. Because silicon is so soft, a single microscopic particle can destroy a chip in production, therefore technology companies spend millions of dollars creating "clean rooms" to protect the chips from contamination. They constantly research ways including the possibility of producing the chips in space, to reduce the number of particles in these rooms.

The human brain is more delicate than silicon. The "particles" that can damage brain functioning are our own internal messages, as well as other people's words, actions, and behaviors that we perceive as threat. For people to realize more of their potential, a leader must create "safe space" for working and learning together— space as free of these negativity "particles" as possible. That's what Annette Griffin does.

The Task of Bringing out the Best in Human Beings and Organizations

As we walked to her car, parked in no particular place at the back of the building, Annette Griffin waved to two maintenance workers standing beside a pickup truck. They smiled broadly and

116

returned her greeting. For the second time this morning, I had the clear sense that people enjoy working here. The first time was when I went to the business office to sign a form. I asked for the name I had been given as a contact and was promptly directed to the right place. A smiling face greeted me, "Hello! I was expecting you to stop by. Here's the form we'd like you to sign." No fumbling through stacks of paper or searching through computer files. The message for me was that in this place, people do quality work.

This was my third visit to the Carrollton-Farmers Branch School District, just north of Dallas. Part of this suburban district—with a student population of over 24,000 and staff of over 2,000—is within the Dallas city limits. But here, I sense none of the strife that has beleaguered some other Dallas area schools in recent years. I was curious about what had created the authentic good will I consistently experienced here.

I decided to ask some questions. "Do you like your job?" I asked the receptionist. "I love it!" she replied. I probed. "Why?" "It's a friendly place," she said. "People really care. They stop to visit and ask how I'm doing." She paused momentarily and comfortably, to reflect. "We smile a lot here—especially Dr. Griffin. No matter what's happening—good or bad—Dr. Griffin smiles, and we know everything is going to be all right. It's very comforting and reassuring."

The receptionist was talking about Dr. Annette Griffin, superintendent of the Carrollton-Farmers Branch School District and Texas Superintendent of the Year for 2000-2001. As if on cue, Annette appeared, her legendary smile glowing from within, ready for our lunch.

Annette Griffin attributes most of her success in life to her parents. She said:

My father was exceptionally gifted, intellectually and athletically. He also had a strong, secure sense of self; he knew who he was. He showed me what was possible. Mother was stability. She let me know I could not do anything that would cause her not to love me. She let me fall and get up.

117

These two standards are a hallmark of Griffin's leadership: set high expectations and accept people for who they are, without judgment, letting them make mistakes. "Part of being great," she says, "is freeing oneself to make mistakes and take risks. I encourage that within the organization. First, I affirm that this is an organization whose goals are linked to a great purpose—producing students who can compete anywhere in the world and have the skills to be of service to their country. Then, through my conversations, my attitude, and my non-verbal communication, I say, 'I accept you. I care about you. I give you the freedom to try.' People need unconditional love in their lives. It releases potential."

An illustration about how Griffin works with people to release their potential is an appointment, earlier in her career, as superintendent for a district wounded by scandal. A television crew had filmed the previous superintendent going into pornographic video stores and houses of prostitution. Reporters came to a board meeting to show the footage, and there was sensational news coverage. People who worked for the organization were very embarrassed. They stopped going to meetings outside the district, where they would be asked humiliating questions. The district went without a leader for a year.

Annette Griffin recalls becoming their leader: "I told them they were great people, doing great things." Gradually, they responded. She explained further:

My challenge was to help them believe in themselves again by affirming them. Four years later, it was very hard for me to leave because they had come so far. I remember the farewell assembly. From the stage, I thanked everyone for the opportunity to make this incredible journey toward hope with them. I celebrated that they had so significantly improved students' achievement that they were out presenting to other school districts. There was a standing ovation to say goodbye. I cried for days because they gave me so much love. It was a celebration of how far they had come, and they knew it.

When she began her career in Richardson, another Dallas suburban school district, Annette Griffin had the opportunity to work with outstanding leaders who recognized her ability to work well with people, her knowledge of how children learn, and her willingness to work hard to get good results. One of these early mentors was Dr. J.J. Pearce, Richardson superintendent, who "asked me to go into a leadership position—even before I was ready. I was only 26 or 27 years old when he appointed me principal. He said, 'Straighten out that school. Get it on the right path.' It was a memorable moment. I even remember what I was wearing on my first day as principal—a red dress with acorns."

Her early mentors gave Griffin quiet assurance of their support and affirmation that she was doing the job well—through notes, words, glances, smiles, touches, and through simply waiting without interfering while she solved problems and met challenges—tools that Griffin continues to use, now that she is the superintendent.

Appreciative Relationships

Griffin's intuitive leadership style keeps her attuned to people's need for learning—and she stays open to new opportunities, mindful that people in organizations take different paths to reach their common goals. She doesn't give up on people.

Terry's story is an example of how Griffin doesn't give up on people. Terry is a middle school principal in Carrollton-Farmers Branch. Trapped by his own fear, he said, "I felt like I had a target on my back." In a reassignment several years earlier, Terry didn't ask some key questions about the reason for the reassignment. Those unasked questions became "what if" ghosts that followed him daily, leaving him wondering, "What if she thinks I can't do my job?" Although no evidence existed to support that theory, Terry's inner doubts were a barrier to reaching his fullest potential.

Griffin learned about a leadership development process designed to release potential, and suggested to Terry that he might apply. He did and was accepted. During the process, a behavioral-style assessment unmasked Terry's fear. Once it surfaced, Terry was able to walk through the fear and to find the truth about his own responsibility for his success. He began to change. Today, he takes more risks. Griffin appreciates Terry's change. "He has a lot more confidence," she says, and she often tells him so.

Even a sensitive, intuitive leader like Griffin is challenged by the diversity of human needs in the large organization she leads. She explains:

Often, people in organizations don't know what they want. They have a vague feeling that all is not well, but they aren't sure why. Sometimes they even blame the top leadership because they aren't getting what they need. My job, as the leader of the organization, is to keep asking questions until people can say what they need. Then, and only then, can we release more of their potential to serve the organization's goals. I like to listen to what people are asking. I'm not afraid to ask people what they want. People within the school system and the larger community come to me for a variety of reasons: information, assistance, reassurance. I listen intently to hear what they want, and then I honor that.

If she can't give people exactly what they ask for, she tells them what she *is* able to do—a strategy she learned from another mentor, retired Richardson Superintendent Arzell Ball. Reflectively, Griffin observes:

Communication is complex; we often misjudge by assuming we know what people want, when we don't. Sometimes they're not even sure. I remember one employee who came to me two or three times, saying she wasn't happy and felt so unfulfilled in her work that she was thinking about leaving. I finally realized that what she wanted was more responsibility. She was bored with a job she had been in too long. When I assigned some other areas to her, she blossomed. I love to see people solve their own problems and realize they had the answer all the time. And a lot of my co-leaders are able to do that, as well.

Griffin's top leadership team is comprised of people who already worked for the school district before Griffin became superintendent. Some had strong loyalty to the previous superintendent. But she describes this leadership team as "the best I've ever had." What did she do to build this team?

120

I assured them we were building a family. I said, "Here's where we're going," and I asked them to help. I talked about vision—culture—hope. I painted a picture with words, and we made a plan. All of us spent time out in the field, listening, finding out where the gaps were. We took action on the gaps first, so that people could see we were moving. We were committed to a single purpose: to create an environment where teachers and principals have the resources to create the best opportunity for each child to achieve in our democracy. We're a service to teachers, to enable them to be their best. We're united behind that common purpose. We're a strong leadership team, even though we didn't choose each other, because we know our purpose, we believe our purpose is worthy, we respect each other, we know our commitment is authentic, and we work as hard as it takes to accomplish our worthy purpose.

Griffin's leadership team learns together. "We read books that I then ask questions about in our team meetings, so that we apply what we're learning to our real situations." One of the books the team has studied together is *Synchronicity: The Inner Side of Leadership*, by Joe Jaworski. Why did Griffin choose that book?

Because of the strife that occurred before I came to Carrollton-Farmers Branch, people had gone into a protective mode. There was a lot of conflict and fear; they were just trying to be safe. As a result, the organization was losing the gift of their creativity. They were not in touch with their souls. I had to touch their souls and sharpen our ability to notice the data the system gives us. Authenticity—being who I am—frees others to be who they are. We are all human beings—capable, loved, and accepted. When this atmosphere prevails, people rise and are able to achieve. I needed to see that change first in the leadership team, where we are authentic with each other. We are caring. We can speak freely about matters of the heart—of the soul—our passions—our gifts. We are comfortable talking about these important aspects of our lives and our work. Our relationship with each other, men and women alike, is rich.

Positive Image and Positive Action

In the organization that Annette Griffin leads, new, dynamic, and compelling positive images of the future come from continuing to learn, listen, and process information. Author Margaret Wheatley says, "Information nourishes a system." Griffin agrees. "In our organization an understood role is that people continue to learn and grow—that we get better. We bring in new information as it meets our needs, to achieve our common purpose that every child graduates with a passion for continuous learning."

Annette believes that a school leader's first responsibility is to show students how to learn and how to create the future they desire. We pay attention and use data to create the future we want. We can create the future in the way we want it to go, from what we choose to focus on. In our organization, we choose to focus on the positive. We understand that each day is a new opportunity in which we can participate fully—contribute fully—live fully. Problems are opportunities. Unfortunately, many people tend to be very self-critical. That's not how we'll become the best human beings we can be. More rapid growth comes from affirming what we do well.

The organization Griffin leads is not immune from the problems that beset so many schools. Recently a high school student, who school leaders later found out was living in a tent behind a discount department store, stole his stepfather's gun, took it to school, and seized one of his classes as hostages. After he had released a few hysterical students, he turned to the teacher, who was pregnant with twins, and told her she could leave. "No," she quietly said. She told the young gunman that she was scared—that she wanted to live to see her babies—but she wanted to help him, too. Then she asked, gently, "How can I help you?" Shortly thereafter, the young man surrendered the gun. No one was hurt.

When the incident occurred, Annette Griffin was at a meeting out of town. How did she feel when she got the call? What did she do? "We had prepared for the possibility of violence, so I was confident in the way it would be handled by the staff and police. I knew it would be handled in a non-confrontational way. I knew the teacher would use her training in working with this troubled child." By the time Griffin returned to the school district, the hostage situation had ended. She went immediately to the school.

"I talked to the faculty and students to celebrate that they had followed procedures so well, that no one was hurt, and the situation was controlled. I stood in the hallways, hugged teachers, and smiled at kids. We worked calmly with the media and used our training." The police said, "They had a plan. They followed their plan. It worked." Nine out of the ten reporters who covered the incident told a positive story.

The Spirit of Inquiry

Probing questions—inquiry—reflection, are the fuels that drive the Griffin-led organizations. In pursuit of helping other people find their truth, she asks these favorite questions:

- What's going on with you?
- How are you taking care of yourself?
- What do you have to celebrate?
- What do you want?
- What do you need?

I like to watch people—listen to them—to find their gifts. Then I affirm, especially their contributions that have gone unnoticed—the strengths they may not have stopped to think through. I affirm their goodness and brilliance—place them in situations where they can use their gifts. Then I watch as their joy of the job grows and creativity blossoms. Over my career, I've seen people, at all levels of organizations, so crippled by their own internal barometers that they cause the climate around them not to function at its best. Gently, with love, I help people uncover what, within them, is causing the problem. Once I worked with an assistant superintendent who believed so passionately about truth, as she knew it. She had to make mistakes before she discovered that truth has to come from within each person. Through using the tools of reflective questioning and listening, more change occurs than by telling people,

"You have to change this immediately!" Telling doesn't work. I invite people to question—to dialogue—to discover ways we've never tried before, so that all children have a chance for success. We use inquiry in almost every interaction in management meetings. Through inquiry, we find better solutions. People rarely say what they really mean in their initial statements. It's important to listen, paraphrase, ask for clarification, delve deeper.

Annette believes leaders must tell their stories—write about them, speak about them, even as they are unfolding. "I tell people why I do things at certain times. I encourage them to ask questions. I'm constantly paying attention, watching for leaders to emerge."

As a mentor for school leaders in Texas, Griffin is well known. She believes that mentoring is a very effective way for leaders to disseminate learnings from their successes. People she mentors can expect her to lead in a way that is congruent with what she says: to give them opportunities—even to put them into tough situations so that they may gain confidence, and to "push them out" when they are ready.

The Role of Positive Affect in Bringing out the Best

Annette's mettle as a leader was forged in her college years. Unlike many educators, she went immediately into graduate school after completing her bachelor's degree. She spent much time in reflection, setting the cornerstones of her value system. "I went to the depths of my soul and the heights of my brain—and I did it purposefully. It was a pivotal time for me." When she left college, she knew whom she was and what her mission was. "I knew that I could do anything—that God would be with me in everything. I knew that no matter what obstacles arose, I would make it—and make it well."

In her mid-twenties, as a newlywed, Annette's faith was closely tested when her father was killed when a propane gas tank exploded. Shortly thereafter, her aunt and uncle were killed in a private plane crash, leaving two small children. Then her mother suffered a stroke. All of this happened within a six-month period. "I had to make a lot of tough decisions. I found I had enough hope and strength to make good decisions. I knew that, with God's help, we would make it—and make it well." But it was the hardest time of her life.

As recently as last summer, Griffin faced another personal crisis with a reaction to a medical prescription. She began having stroke-like symptoms.

One night I felt as if I might not make it through the night. I lay there, feeling joy for the life I've had. I felt confident that my family would make it—and make it well. I felt hope for tomorrow and gratitude for the opportunities I've had in this life. Until people get in touch with a Higher Being or Power, they are not free enough to be who they really are. As people begin to understand this wonderful world, they gain a sense of appreciation, awe, and humility as they find the place they are meant to be—where they are most fulfilled—where they find most meaning. There's a zone that is higher when people have appreciation and awe that allows them to be part of the unfolding of this wonderful world.

Griffin talks freely with her leadership team about matters of the soul. Does she find any difference in the ability of men and women to deal with such issues? "Not at all. When we are able to give love—to look at another person with all we have and all we want to give, there's a unique level of consciousness. It's freeing ourselves to release the soul within us that never dries up—never stops giving, loving, expecting, forgiving; it's having an oasis within that is always abundant."

I was curious about the oasis Annette described—a place within, so abundant that it never dries up and is always able to give. I wondered what sustains the oasis. How does she nourish and replenish the oasis within her? She didn't hesitate. "Prayer. Reflection. Sitting and watching water. Listening to the still, quiet voice. And, every day, asking God to give me the opportunity to be of service."

Gratitude powers Annette Griffin's positive affect in her life and work—and she is a learner. She constantly sets goals to learn something new and accomplish something different. Her latest

125

ambitions are to learn to speak Spanish and to play golf. But she confesses:

> I haven't found balance in my life. I'm so passionate about what I do as a school leader that I often take time away from my family, from exercise and a nutritious diet, even from reflection and meditation, in order to do my job. And the thing I really wish I did more is to celebrate in my own life. I constantly feel grateful for opportunities, but I rarely have a feeling of accomplishment. In fact, recognition and affirmation are difficult for me to accept for myself. What I would say to leaders is to look for affirmative feedback— for the valuable information that the organization is giving them—that affirms that they are doing the job well. I encourage appreciative leaders to give themselves the love that they share so freely with others.

Chapter Five

Reflections of a Lifetime

Three wise ones describe facets of their deeply pledged lives. James "Dolph" Norton, a near octogenerian, demonstrates cognitive and emotional nimbleness as he moves through eight high-profile responsibilities as president or chancellor in higher education. He shows us how he has accomplished much based on a strong, long-held belief that he is capable of all that is being asked of him. Bernard "Doc" Lafayette, is currently Distinguished Scholar-in-Residence and Director of the Center for Nonviolence and Peace Studies at the University of Rhode Island. He tells passionate stories of his commitment to nonviolent desegregation, beginning in Selma, Alabama in 1961. Warren Bennis, Distinguished Professor of Business Administration, University of Southern California, has been central in shaping the global dialogue on leadership. He speaks from both the process and theory of leadership. In this chapter, Bennis reflects on his own experiences on being a leader.

As three women editors we chose these three leaders, not to exclude women's ways but to share wisdom from three very special people.

The Eternal Optimist:
James A. "Dolph" Norton

Dr. James A. Norton, Emeritus President, Central Washington University, Ellensburg, Washington

Linda C. Winner
and Jeffrey A. Doyle

James A. (Dolph) Norton has served as a Professor at Florida State University; Executive Director of Cleveland Metropolitan Services Commission; Director of The Cleveland Foundation; Director of the University of Virginia Center for Public Service; and Chancellor or President of eight universities and higher education systems. He has a BA from Louisiana State University and an MA and PhD from Harvard University.

He says he is an old man now, only a year and a half from eighty. But if you reviewed his career over the past twelve years you would not know it. He's what some university governing boards call a "savior": someone who is asked to serve and save learning institutions in difficult times and quietly leave once the crisis is averted and the institution is back on its feet. In June 2000, he completed his sixth different position since 1988 as President or Chancellor of a college, university, or higher education system. In one difficult instance, he was asked to serve as President after the former President and the entire university's Governing Board were removed by the state Board of Regents. Few could survive, let alone prosper, in such difficult leadership roles. Dolph Norton, however, welcomes these roles.

James A. (Dolph) Norton was born and raised in Louisiana during the Great Depression. After serving in the U.S. Army during World War II, he completed his bachelor's degree at Louisiana State University. By 1950, Norton had both an MA and PhD from Harvard and, in six years' time, progressed from Assistant to Associate to Full Professor of Public Administration at Florida State

University. In 1956, he took on a totally new challenge and served as Executive Director of the Cleveland Metropolitan Service Commission. By 1963, he had transitioned to Director of the Cleveland Foundation, a position he used to direct the disbursement of millions of dollars to philanthropic and civic projects. By the early 1970's the Foundation, under Dolph Norton's leadership, had such a major impact on the community that he was called the "second most powerful man in all of Cleveland" by the largest, local daily newspaper (the most powerful man being Mayor Carl Stokes).

After finishing his tenure at the Cleveland Foundation, Norton began a period of 27 years in which he served as President or Chancellor of such institutions as Case Western Reserve University, Central Washington University, the Ohio Board of Regents (responsible for 61 public campuses in Ohio), and the University of Maryland System (11 campuses and four research centers). In addition to his six honorary doctorates from colleges and universities and many other civic and academic honors, Norton served as President of the American Society for Public Administration and the Chair of the Board of the National Academy of Public Administration.

Lofty titles and impressive accomplishments are only part of Dolph Norton's story of leadership. The people who worked for him tell an even greater story. For example, Daryl Greer, Director of the New Jersey Council of State University Trustees, states: "In my 25 years of working in higher education, I have never met a leader more democratic or nurturing, open and giving, than Dolph." Tom Albert, Director of Ethnic Outreach for the Democratic National Committee, believes: "Everything I know about leadership and working with people I learned from Dolph." Lou Starkey, former Provost at Adelphi University, believes that Dolph Norton demonstrates, "the best-ever example of moral character." Margaret Drugovich, a university vice-president, states, "No one in my professional life holds a candle to Dolph in his ability to work with people." Many of Norton's protégés noted that they would have neither earned their doctorates nor stayed in higher education we it not not for his encouragement and support.

Dolph is a humble man, often described as a leader who never attempts to prove he is a leader; he demonstrates his leadership by what the organization or institution accomplishes. Dolph's humility makes it difficult to interview him, because he speaks as if his knowledge is common sense and anyone else would do the same things in his place.

For almost the last twenty years one of the writers of this piece has known Dolph as his junior colleague, assistant, member of his staff, observer, and dear friend. She has seen him in good times and bad, elated with successes and frustrated by the lack of them, bursting with new ideas and remembering old formulas. She has heard him quote the Scotsman Bruce that "he'll lay him down and bleed awhile and then he'll fight again," and seen the value he gives to persistence. But she's never heard him explain his theory of what he does to bring out the best in everyone with whom he works. Interviewing Dolph Norton has allowed her to learn how--as well as why--he has been such a successful leader and mentor.

Bringing out the Best in Human Beings and Organizations

The first step in Dolph's plan, to bring out the best in people, is built on his acceptance of the talents everyone brings, no matter how big or small. He is not concerned with someone's lofty title or position in the hierarchy; he wants people around him who think differently from him and are not afraid to ask tough questions. Norton is a keen judge of people's abilities and was described by one of his former vice presidents as having "an intuitive sense of people." In Dolph's words, "You recruit the best people you can find and let them know that you think they are the best." Once Dolph has assembled a cast of intelligent and hard working people, he identifies their specific talents and helps them find projects or positions in which their talents will be most useful.

A great example of this occurred when a graduate student, John Olsen, in the mid-1960's wrote a paper on the Economic Opportunity Act of 1964. Dolph Norton was Director of the Cleveland Foundation; at the same time he was teaching and was preparing for a United States Congressional Committee to visit Cleveland and study local economic opportunity issues in the area.

Norton recognized Olsen's insights, and asked him to prepare an integrated approach to economic development for Cleveland. Norton and Olsen agreed that the city needed an overarching vision based on collaboration and sharing resources. When the members of the Congressional Committee heard the presentation they were overwhelmed and ecstatic. No other city was taking the type of approach the Cleveland Foundation was recommending. Norton was asked to present the economic development framework to the full Congressional Committee. Norton saw the potential in Olsen and found a way to make it possible for him to contribute. Olsen, who since has served as vice president in several organizations, attributes a large part of the project's success to Norton's lack of ego, his understanding of the political dynamics at work, and his refusal to use, what Olsen called, "the power of the elite."

In addition to identifying the gifts of each person, Dolph wants to know that all his employees have a strong belief in the mission of the organization. If he trusts individuals' desires to work toward something greater than themselves, he gives them ownership for tasks that might seem greater than they can handle. One of Dolph's former staff members in the early 1970's was asked to interview the mayor of Akron, Ohio, on an issue of importance to the Cleveland Foundation. It didn't matter to him that the staff member was a 23-year old intern, straight out of college. Dolph believes in people's potential. When the intern doubted his ability to complete the interview, Dolph saw it as a personal responsibility to convince the intern that he was the best person for the job and that his contribution was critical. Dolph Norton's inner confidence in people's abilities often convinces them that they are ready for the task he has given them.

Norton likes to set "reach goals"--goals that may seem difficult to achieve without superhuman effort. Once these goals are set, he challenges people to use their abilities to cross boundaries, go beyond their job descriptions, and give whatever effort it takes to accomplish them. As he sets the pace with his own hard work, he also guides and supports those working with him by continually recognizing their contributions. Dolph often acknowledges accomplishments in public settings, where he can demonstrate to the person being recognized that he is so proud of his or her work that he wants to tell others about it. He does not give "fake praise" as one former employee stated. When he gives a compliment he sincerely means it and wants the recipient to know it.

As Norton grew as a leader, his supervisors used public recognition to help him feel valued. He appreciated it when his bosses did not take sole credit for projects, but used "we" to communicate what the entire team had done to achieve success. Dolph's mentors often treated him as a peer and maintained lifelong relationships with him. Dolph has returned this favor by staying in touch with many of the individuals he has mentored over the years. He counts many of these people as his friends, and their respect for him is immense. Many visit him regularly. For example, a former colleague recently took two days off from her current position as a university vice president to fly to his home and discuss professional growth issues. After patiently listening to her describe one of her key challenges, he helped her conceptualize the confusing issue in seconds, leaving her amazed at his ability to identify the critical element in the midst of a mass of information.

Appreciative Relationships

Dolph's belief in abundant feedback drives his leadership style in many ways. His definition of feedback includes that which he offers and that which he receives from others. "Blue-sky lunches," times when he can gather people from all reaches of the organizational hierarchy to listen to and understand their insights, are common. "Yes people" are not the people Norton wants around him; he wants people with all types of viewpoints who are not afraid to be honest with him. One of Norton's former vice presidents noted, "People never have to fear being vulnerable with Dolph," because he deeply respects authentic people who share their minds. As Norton puts it, "An open and accepting atmosphere will make it possible for your 'subordinates' to identify criticisms of your performance and to make suggestions that they believe will help the organization."

An excellent example of Dolph Norton's willingness to build relationships that open the door to feedback occurred when he replaced a president who had designated the university-owned president's house as private and virtually off-limits to university employees. Soon after settling in, Norton began to host regular gatherings of faculty, staff, and students at his new home. He welcomed visitors and made sure that no one felt uncomfortable talking to him at home or at the office.

Dolph ensures that people have access to him. When he serves as a university president, students are frequent visitors, not because they are required to see him but because they feel welcomed. He is famous for remembering students' names and details about their lives. He is known to personalize his speeches on important issues with anecdotes about the students with whom he has been talking. Many of Norton's protégés mention the investment of time he makes in people. These people attribute much of their professional success to Norton's willingness to trust their abilities and offer them opportunities to succeed in significant projects. Several of these people describe Dolph Norton's desire to help young people succeed as the trait they try most to emulate in their professional lives.

Another avenue Norton uses to create appreciative relationships occurs through regular private meetings with people to whom he has delegated responsibility. Norton brings a very loose agenda with him, because he wants to have the freedom to discuss anything that may be important to his staff. In addition, because of his genuine interest in people, he tries to engage them in discussions of their interests.

Dolph also likes to visit people in their offices. He believes this shows his respect for their positions and his willingness to meet them where they are most comfortable. By visiting people's offices around campus, he also gets to further interact with students and observe the moods people create in their workplaces. Norton does not like to communicate through his support staff. His visits to offices are opportunities for him to establish personal contact. To Dolph, personal relationships are the entrée to collaboration and cooperation.

This ability to leave his office and "get out" does not come without a cost. Norton is dependent on his support staff for organizing and balancing all of the many projects he constantly juggles. All good leaders have weaknesses, and the really great leaders know their weaknesses and find ways of compensating for them. Norton is careful to surround himself with staff members that provide the structure he needs in a multi-tasking environment. As one of Norton's former employees puts it, "Dolph would rather be juggling eight balls and drop four of them, than to carefully juggle just one ball." For example, while he was at the Cleveland Foundation, several groups wanted to meet with him for breakfast on the same day. Norton thought that these groups shared some common interests, but he needed to take the time for separate breakfast sessions to understand each of them. Norton ended up with one breakfast meeting at 6:30 a.m., one at 9:00 a.m., and a brunch at 11:00 a.m. As one of Dolph's assistants at the time mentioned, "He didn't have to do that. He didn't get paid to do that. And the other amazing thing is that he did that without any appreciable weight gain!"

Dolph believes, "Collaboration in the abstract is nonsense." He insists that collaboration is most successful when it is built around an issue with a direct impact on the people involved. By focusing on shared resolutions to the issue, competing groups become less aware of their personal differences and more intent on teamwork. It is important, however, that success on the issue be measurable without extraordinary time and effort. The leader must help set goals that are realistic and achievable by considering the groups being asked to collaborate.

One of Norton's colleagues has vivid memories of Dolph's encouragement of collaboration among mayors and city managers who were divided by race and other issues. Norton had invited them to cooperate in solving regional resource problems, but they were spending most of their time defining the things they were not going to do. After about 30 unconstructive minutes, Dolph stood up. In his deep, bass voice, he told them that he did not invite them with the expectation that they would leave liking each other, but he did expect that they would work together to solve some of the issues facing them. The tone of the meeting was different from that point forward.

Positive Images and Actions

Norton's efforts at encouraging collaboration are often avenues for creating positive images for the future. Time and again, Dolph's friends and protégés identified "leadership by inclusion" as one of his greatest strengths. "If you don't use every person or group to come up with a positive image of the future, you've wasted an important resource," he says. "Positive images of the future can originate anywhere without any regard for the [person's] level of responsibility. There is a dynamism in daily living: changing environments, new problems, changing interactions among individuals, old thoughts being refined, and so on."

Dolph also welcomes diversity of thinking: "Chances are that the broader a person's perspective, the greater the knowledge base, the more creativity that is likely to be coming."

Norton's predecessor in one of his university presidencies was known for his secrecy and failure to share information: a camera had been installed outside the President's office to view any visitors; the doors to the President's offices were always kept locked; and important financial information was kept locked in the office. When Norton arrived he immediately had the camera turned off and the doors unlocked. He placed the financial information, which had aroused great curiosity, in the university library for all to see. Then he invited the university community to review the information and visit him with any positive ideas they had for improvement. This process exemplifies Norton's belief that information empowers people and helps them reach their full potential, which in turn makes the organization more successful.

In Norton's view, a leader's job of facilitating cooperation is not about collecting information, rather, it's about actively participating in stimulating and encouraging creative thinking. According to those who have worked with him, he never criticizes an idea. When he hears an idea that might appear off-track or far-fetched, he responds with, "Let's think about that one for a while," or, "What if we thought about that this way?" In Dolph's words, "Skilled leaders, I believe, have to make sure there is an accepting atmosphere for good—and bad—ideas so that the best can be captured and supported. Negative feedback will soon diminish the output. An appreciative attitude for every suggestion will encourage people."

At times, Norton has been criticized for acting on issues more slowly than others have thought he should. However, he firmly believes in allowing a problem to emerge fully and be articulated clearly before beginning to build a consensus for solutions. When everyone understands the problem and issues involved, potential solutions make sense to more people and are implemented more easily. By taking time to encourage buy-in on significant issues, Dolph builds group responsibility for issues: "The genius of group responsibility in organizations is that it helps provide a fertile field for new ideas and a sounding board to make sure that the new project gets a fair hearing."

When positive images emerge from groups, Dolph Norton believes that they represent widely shared interests and ideas that need to be acted upon. Too often, Dolph sees new ideas vanish "in the myriad of filters that society provides--some individual, some organizational, and some just in the noise of living." To maintain the energy level needed to act on positive images, he tries to balance challenging others and celebrating with them each step of the way.

When asked if he is a positive thinker in his own life, Dolph's answer is unsurprisingly brief. "Be an optimist," he suggests. And when he realizes this might not be enough information he adds, "Sometimes when I get down, I come up with the idea that we literally have no choice but to succeed. So let's go ahead and do something."

The Spirit of Inquiry

The "something" that Norton spent a lot of time doing was developing a spirit of inquiry among his colleagues. He believes that inquiry must be one the organization's goals. He is constantly asking questions, including, "What are we doing? How well are we doing it? What is our next step?" One of Norton's former graduate students, who went on to become a vice president for a bank and a higher education system, describes how Dolph Norton makes people feel valued by the manner in which he inquires. "An excellent listener who acts on the advice he receives, Dolph is not one of those 'leaders' who listens with interest to everything that is said, agrees with it all, promises action, and delivers nothing. He listens with interest to everything that is said, takes the advice to heart and acts on it, and then gives the credit for success to the people who generated the original idea."

Dolph tells the stories of past organizational achievements in order to replicate learning from success. He is careful to emphasize that people should talk about what was done right, not wrong, in the past. By remembering positive lessons, people are more likely to repeat them in the future. He also likes to bring in outside groups or persons to study what his organization or institution is doing. Often the results of this consultation include the development of new ideas and the confirmation of many excellent ideas already being implemented.

In spite of Dolph's efforts to emphasize past successes, he never characterizes organizational achievements as if they were due to his leadership. Several of his protégés mentioned his "lack of ego," in that Norton did not need to feel important in order to be successful. "He doesn't make you feel as if it is his show as so many other leaders have a tendency to do," remarked one of his former staff members. For example, Norton asked a young intern to attend the meeting of a special interest group which had just received a very large grant from the Cleveland Foundation. Although the group accepted the grant, the meeting devolved from harsh criticism to slander of the Foundation's leadership. When Norton asked the young man how the meeting had gone, the intern fearfully reported the disgust and hatred expressed toward both the Cleveland Foundation and Norton, in spite of the generous grant. He expected Norton to get angry. Instead, he looked at the young man and calmly replied, "We should never expect appreciation just because we are the people who get to give away the money. We have been appointed to do a job, and we will do it as well as we can."

Most of the time, people really like any job with which Dolph Norton is associated. One of the reasons for this is that Norton focuses on both developing a good process and attaining a positive outcome. He usually asks groups he is leading to identify the outcome first, and then work backward to determine the best process for achieving the outcome. By having a clear understanding of the final goal, it is more evident how to best proceed toward this goal. He has frequently relied on this skill during his eight higher education presidencies and chancellorships; and his success has been remarkable. At one university he changed the culture of the President's office to make it a welcoming and enjoyable place to work, balanced the university's budget for the first time in several years, and turned around declining enrollments.

The Role of Positive Affect

Dolph recognized that these institutions needed a sense of hope. In his words, "I needed to help people realize that there are better days ahead, we are all in this together, and this is something we enjoy." In the words of one of Dolph's former vice presidents, "There is simply a joy that emanates from him. It's the essence of who he is." Even in dire situations, Dolph is known to lift his head up and declare, "Let the good times roll." This eternal optimism inspired his colleagues at these "institutions-in-transition" to trust his belief that things would get better.

This optimism does not, however, brand Norton as a cheerleader. He does not motivate everyone with his excitement and energy and then allow them to burn out. He resembles the tortoise more than the hare, and is described by his former employees as someone who lives his values and takes time every day to validate those with whom he comes in contact.

Reflecting on some of the most ambitious projects with which he has been associated, Dolph shared how his sense of optimism was proportional to the importance of the project. For example, when working on Civil Rights issues in the early 1970's, Dolph explained how it was essential to believe that something positive could be done. "We hoped, even against hope, that we might succeed or that there would be some successes worthy of the risk....How great it has been to share in the sense that we were engaged in something of real consequence."

The defining moment of Dolph Norton's leadership journey occurred in his 30's when, as Executive Director of Cleveland

Metropolitan Services Commission, he was meeting with his supervisor every week to discuss progress on their projects. Unfortunately, the Commission's projects had many more problems than accomplishments and Norton's boss wanted him to demonstrate more results in shorter time. One night Dolph was having a church group meeting at his home and shared his challenges at work with a friend. On learning the name of Dolph's boss, the friend declared, "Do you have any idea how many people your boss has given heart attacks to?" At first Dolph wondered how long it would be until he too was driven to some sort of medical emergency. Later that night, however, he thought to himself, "I'll be damned if I'm going to have a heart attack because of this guy. I'm going to drive him crazy rather than the other way around." From that day on Dolph took greater initiative on his projects and decided that he was going to tackle problems head on and not look back. His new optimistic and proactive attitude surprised his boss who was supportive from that moment on. Dolph's lesson in this story was not that he needed to take a vacation or work less, but that he needed to change his internal mindset from one of allowing himself to be discouraged about problems to one of believing that he could accomplish all that was being asked of him.

Looking back on the ups and downs of his leadership career, Dolph offers one lesson he learned over time: "A leader should never stay in one position for too long." The problem, as he sees it, is that leaders can lose their ability to see the real problems. Over time most leaders surround themselves with people with whom they are comfortable and they lose their willingness to imagine and create. Dolph tries to avoid "growing stale" and is always willing to try new things, even at the age of 78. The variety of many jobs in his career path certainly makes this clear.

Sometimes people have a tendency to assume that leaders who reach high positions must have always been aiming there. According to Norton, he never knew where his career was going; he was merely trying to take new challenges, do his best, and be successful. The analogy he uses is one of Tarzan in the jungle, swinging from vine to vine. Although Tarzan may have known where he was going, he never knew which vine he would grab next until he was ready to let go of the one he was holding. When he finally let go of a vine, there always seemed to be another one that he could grab onto. "I never ended up on the ground," Dolph declares.

Dolph Norton is a wonderful example of a person whose eternal optimism has propelled him to amazing heights and instilled in him a leadership style that motivates all those around him to believe in a brighter future. Dolph's honesty and integrity have made him a leadership model for hundreds of people who have met and interacted with him over the years. His leadership style has nothing to do with the best way to play politics or manipulate others. While describing a difficult situation he encountered during a presidency, he explained, "I knew they had politics; I just chose to ignore them." The "Eternal Optimist" strikes again.

Little Gandhi Continues To March

Bernard LaFayette, Jr., Distinguished-Scholar-in-Residence and Director, The Center for Nonviolence and Peace Studies, University of Rhode Island, Kingston, Rhode Island

Gene Knott

Bernard LaFayette, Jr. has been a Civil Rights activist, minister, and educator on nonviolent social change. He co-founded the Student Nonviolent Coordinating Committee (SNCC) in 1960, and was a leader in the Selma Voter Registration Project, the Southern Christian Leadership Conference (SCLC), and the Poor Peoples' Campaign. He received his EdD from Harvard, and currently is Distinguished-Scholar-in-Residence and Director of the Center for Nonviolence and Peace Studies at the University of Rhode Island.

Each time a person stands up for an ideal, or acts to improve the lot of others, or strikes out against injustice, they send forth a tiny ripple of hope.   Robert F. Kennedy

    When the 19th-century poet Arthur O'Shaughnessy spoke of leaders as "movers and shakers," he could have been referring to the life work of the man who, as a 21-year-old student activist in the 1960's, was labeled "Little Gandhi" by Mississippi cellmate and fellow Freedom Rider, James Farmer. Bernard LaFayette, Jr., is affectionately known as "Doc." An energetic, yet gentle and quietly impressive man, he is also a naturally engaging storyteller. LaFayette's own story is eloquently chronicled in David Halberstam's (1998) book, *The Children*, a marvelous narrative of the courage and deeds of the young people and their leaders who desegregated the southern U.S. in a nonviolent manner beginning in the 1960's.

    Dr. LaFayette held me spellbound for over two hours, pausing between commitments that day as campus educator and chair of the Rhode Island Select Commission on Race and Police

Community Relations. A frequent lecturer and trainer all over the globe, Bernard LaFayette, Jr. ranged over his experiences of followership and leadership since his birth in Tampa, Florida, in 1940. He described with a twinkling eye and calming, warm smile the lessons he tries to impart today about the truly appreciative character of nonviolent social change.

LaFayette said that the first thing he looks for in leaders is "openness to differences!" If their expressed ideas and shared perspectives give me a sense of their strength, that is, they can truly function as a leader and not simply fill the role as figurehead, then that shows me real promise, the possibility of making good things happen." He went on to note his belief that some organizations become very narrow and really get into hero-worship. "For example," he noted, "some church groups in my experience are dictatorships, and that behavior handicaps the organization and prevents its people from really experiencing their best...;it thwarts the true mission of the group. Real leaders have genuine followers in the sense that they are all pulling willfully in the same direction; that's how I hear author Peter Drucker's statement that leadership is creating an alignment of strengths that negates individual weaknesses."

An ordained minister and former seminary faculty member, as well as former president of the American Baptist College Seminary in Nashville, and former Dean of the Graduate School of Alabama State University in Montgomery, Dr. LaFayette can speak from wide and deep experiences as both churchman and leader. He referred frequently to the leadership lessons learned in the summer of 1962, when he volunteered to head a voter registration project in Selma, Alabama. He was guided by Rufus Lewis, a local educator and coach, who understood both the challenging environment there for Blacks, and the plotting, local, White officials they' d encounter.

He referred to Rufus Lewis as a wise and knowledgeable leader of the drive for all citizens' rights. "He tutored me on techniques to get voters registered, to enroll them in groups. He knew when to do what and when to hold back—a mentor for the time and my needs!" One of the lessons Lewis taught LaFayette was that you have to assess the prospects of followership.

He said it was like finding oil in the ocean! You have to do your homework and know what approaches and what people work best under what conditions and in what locations. It wasn't like we went in there blind altogether. I had written a 50-page paper on the existing leadership in Dallas County, Alabama before going in.

LaFayette likened collaboration to a "best practices" approach to voter enrollment. Local leadership was the key to getting the Southern Christian Leadership Conference (SCLC) and the Student Nonviolent Coordinating Committee (SNCC) working together. He demurred, "I just stimulated their collaboration with one another, so the outsiders and the locals could come together to achieve the goals of the drive. It was a combination of letting the people decide, along with trusting that I was someone with a positive history and principles that they could respect."

This was a stellar example of several key appreciative leadership characteristics and the relationships such behavior can engender—encouraging the best in people to enable them to partner toward a higher outcome, using mutual feedback and listening. "All the time listening," Doc emphasized, "to what they—the disenfranchised of the area—had to say about their needs, their wants, and their willingness to cooperate."

And further adding to their sense of shared resolve was that their office, the place they met most nights, was situated right across the street from the Selma jail, frequented by the most feared and militant official in the county, a strident segregationist county sheriff. "We bonded under that threat," said Doc. It was an atmosphere that created unity out of a frustration, with shared hopelessness being turned into the prospect of recognition and empowerment.

When all were equally threatened, the threat became a common bond that fortified us. And, on the surface, we were not a very powerful-seeming collection of individuals: there were seven of us—"The Magnificent Seven"—a postal worker, our hostess Mrs. Boynton, two school teachers, a dental assistant, a lawyer, and me! Why, they were demonstrating courage just being associated with me! They could've been killed—it was a dangerous situation.

143

He continued:

> One of the best decisions we made that summer was to make sure that we didn't look too much like outside interveners. So we decided not to create a new organization to mobilize for voting rights, but instead I became a staff member of an already existing organization dedicated to the same goals, the County Voters' League. That meant I was a staff member of an organization led by adult members of the citizenry. And thereby, we accomplished several important things: we avoided the interloper appearance, we built on what was already in place that was at least passively tolerated if not accepted, and we forged a working alliance on the blending of several people's ideas, talents, and dedication. That saved us a lot of time and probably avoided a lot of early confrontation too.

Here is how Doc was described in Halberstam's book:

> He seemed to put other people, no matter what their backgrounds, at ease. Socially he was relaxed and nimble. If he was at war with the segregated environment, then he was in no way at war with himself. On the surface he appeared almost carefree. But the commitment was there and it was deep and it was driven by religious faith.

Doc said, "For some, nonviolence was a tactic, but for leaders in the movement it was a way of life!"

I mentioned to him that I often say to my Organization Development students: "Leaders are born, made, and called upon." In response, Doc said that, from his youngest days, at age seven in his grandmother's living room where he was referred to as the "little Preacher," he could talk to groups of adults, lead them in singing hymns, and generally be a leader by example and by sharing his deeply felt beliefs. "By the way," he mentioned, "my grandmother started that church in her house with just a handful of worshippers. That small enterprise grew to be a couple thousand parishioners in a matter of just a few years!" So LaFayette had a powerful example early on of what a patient and focused leader could accomplish with a clear vision and commitment.

A member of the NAACP Youth Council as a schoolboy, president of various youth groups as he grew up, treasurer of the Ambassadors—a group of church ushers who attended to more than merely seating parishioners--and editor of his college yearbook, all are testimony to Doc's belief that you lead more by what you do than by what you say. "Leadership development is one of my main things—to find volunteers and professionals who will give leadership to the important work of organizations." Doc defines such leadership as "the ability to recruit followers who share your ideals, and are willing to work toward their realization." When he was a neophyte in the Civil Rights movement, he said he took extensive mental notes about how Dr. Martin Luther King, Jr., and other leaders of the movement functioned in those roles. LaFayette spoke as if he were not among them as a leader, a position history does not support.

As noted earlier, Doc is an inveterate and gifted storyteller, a man whose teaching talents emerge from the amalgam of this gift with his passion for his beliefs. "I teach by sharing my experiences, and by helping people to identify current issues. Learning how to apply stories is not just intellectual education, but emotional learning as well." He remarked that the songs, the music of the human rights' movements throughout the world, are themselves lyric storytelling. "They articulate the aspirations, the goals of those efforts at setting people free to be, to become their best selves." So creating followership is first a matter of shared ideals, then of hard work in collaboration toward one's goals—a clear paraphrase of Appreciative Inquiry.

He shared the analogy of the difference between a thermometer and a thermostat: The former merely takes the temperature, while the latter is like a leader. "It sets the temperature, it moves us to change," he said with a knowing smile of assurance. I asked Dr. LaFayette if he was familiar with Thomas Paine's famous utterance, "Prejudice will fall in a combat with interest." LaFayette opined that some people fail to see their own interest as a shared one. "Only when they taste defeat do some persons come to see an alternative truth."

He went on to say:

The toughest part of teaching as a leader is getting others to recognize that they share goals in common. Once that happens, it's easy to find others with the right complement of skills to accomplish the desired results. I admire Martin Luther King most for creating leaders. He did it not just by associating and showing the way, but also by teaching. I recall him asking in many groups the simple question, 'What is power?' He'd listen awhile and then he'd say it was simply the ability to achieve purpose. And, despite the personal power and charisma of the man, he was a master at getting followership because of shared ideals, not a cult of personality. That's why the movement endures; it's based on principles, not the presence of certain people.

I was reminded of the lessons described in Bennis and Biederman's book, *Organizing Genius*, about how so-called "great groups" came about and are sustained. They point out that leadership comes in many guises and from many places, and often the visible leader is only one of many. It takes different leadership styles working in concert to pull off great endeavors, lasting accomplishments. Doc said reflectively, "Leaders in the movement had to be both authentic and accepting if they hoped to succeed, if they wanted to gain followers! Without a lot of communication and building on a range of different groups and their differing skills, a 381-day boycott would have been impossible to pull off!"

Dr. LaFayette pursued the theme of positive image and positive action further, noting, "The Quakers had long had nonviolent groups and teachings and they used volunteers. Leaders in the Civil Rights movement had a similar idea, but what was new was the combination of union organizing strategies, of putting ourselves in harm's way, and we gained support from the labor movement. Local Blacks in the South cooperated with outside Whites, and over time, also picked up Southern Whites who worked elsewhere." These coalitions and this growth were the "critical mass" of the movement, according to LaFayette.

I asked him to cite a high point for him, a moment when he thought his example as leader brought out the best in people. After a short pause, he replied, "I'd go back to that experience the summer of '62 in Selma. Those people said that I gave them hope, knowing that even under the threat of being killed, they felt that what we were doing and how we were going about it, was right...and timely. We really felt that we were making a small contribution to the country right there in Alabama; a step toward changing attitudes, changing racism."

I read a quote from Aristotle: "A vivid imagination compels the whole body to obey it!" Doc looked up after glancing at his desk for a moment, and remarked: "Identify the goal you seek, yes. But, idealism is only meaningful if you can have tangible results, concrete outcomes, and accomplishments."

Moving toward the finish of our time together, I pressed again on the theme of "appreciative leadership," asking LaFayette about his own difficult lessons when in the role of point person. He said, "One of the hardest things for me to learn—and I think it's a problem for a lot of leaders—was that I had to show more diplomacy, and not just speak my mind." He noted further that both tact and avoidance of bridge burning were important if a person truly wanted to lead over the long term.

LaFayette had done a reprise of sorts just a month before this interview at a campus concert headlined by Pete Seeger. Seeger called him on stage late in the show and referred to having first met Bernard LaFayette when they performed a program together at Carnegie Hall decades before. He broke into a self-conscious smile, adding, "I was not a singer, but I could harmonize well. That's what we did in the (Nashville) Quartet." This night, Doc regaled the packed house with lyrics made up and sung in a Mississippi jail, and joined Seeger and his son-in-law for a medley of songs from the '60's, songs written for and about the Civil and Human Rights movement. And he was in fine voice, and did indeed harmonize well!

LaFayette also spoke about the importance of giving as a leader:
Since I was seven or eight, I'd contributed to the household by delivering coffee. This was before kitchen coffeemakers, and way before Starbucks. Back then, I'd go buy coffee for some neighbors and merchants in a three-block area near home, and I'd deliver it to them in the morning. It

only cost ten cents back then, and I'd usually get a generous ten cent tip. That was a lot then; I'd gather enough money for others in the family too, enough to buy them a head-to-toe outfit. So, I've always felt that a part of responsibility to others included the need to give back. That's essential to leadership—to contribute back to humanity, not just the country. You're part of the world!

He asked if I was familiar with the saying, "You should be ashamed to die until you strike a blow...to make a difference for humanity." This notion of global service to humankind is part of what has Bernard LaFayette traveling all over the world these days, talking and teaching about these things that he believes in so dearly, these things that have been the whole of his life.

In the eye of this beholder, Dr. Bernard LaFayette, Jr., has been a lifelong leader of change in every way we have come to characterize good leadership, Appreciative Leadership. He has done so in the most basic system seeking change—in our relationships as fellow human beings!

Warren Bennis: An Appreciative Thought And Action Leader

Warren Bennis, Distinguished Professor of Business Administration, University of Southern California, Los Angeles, California

Bea Mah Holland

Acclaimed leadership expert Warren Bennis is a University of Southern California professor, author, former infantry commander, university president, and provost. His best selling books include Leaders, *and* On Becoming a Leader. Forbes Magazine *refers to him as the "Dean of Leadership Gurus."*

We are all angels with only one wing, we can fly only while embracing each other.   Luciano De Crescenzo

I first encountered Dr. Warren Bennis's work in 1986. With a newly minted doctorate in hand, I joined Digital Equipment Corporation, now Compaq. During my first week, I was assigned a role teaching managers about leadership in a week-long residential program, using Bennis and Burt Nanus's (1985) book, *Leaders: The Strategies for Taking Charge*, a classic that has been translated into 13 languages. In the fall of 2001 my co-editors and I had a conversation with Warren Bennis. During that day with Bennis, we felt that we were in the presence of a cultivator of people and someone who walked his talk. With us, he lived out his articulated aspirations—to be remembered as one who personally touched individual lives.

Warren Bennis spoke about three requirements needed for bringing out the best in humans individually and collectively: 1) a group of people who feel a true obligation to know and understand each other; 2) a leader who models this; and 3) a shared belief that the task is one in which the heart is engaged and one that will have a positive impact on the world.

149

In acknowledging the first condition, he talked about the importance of being known and knowing, and related a story about a situation when he had been president of the University of Cincinnati. He came to see how, despite "knowing" a staff person for several years, he had never embraced this man as a whole person. When he participated in an exercise where partners were instructed to really look at each other, he saw this person's "pathos, the worry lines" for the first time. Using language such as "opaque and guarded" to describe the more common *modus operandi*, he went on to advise, "Be authentic, be available and more open, and feel others' wholeness."

As a leader, Warren Bennis acknowledged the need to know and be known by others, his second factor. He spoke about showing vulnerability and legitimating doubt. "Leaders and the led are the most intimate allies in the most powerful partnership." In a recent interview for the *LA Times*, he said, "I don't think a leader can be great unless there's a symbiosis between the leader and the led. Everything I've observed over the last 45 years is that leaders are made great by their people and their people are made great by leaders."

The third factor, that the work needs to be engaging and important, is rooted in the desire of people to partake in "a mission that will make a dent in the world beyond what any one [person] can do." The leader's work is to manage the dream, to remind people what is important and how they are creating the difference. In an *Industry Week* article, "Cultivating Creative Genius," Bennis retells the story related by the late Nobel-Prize winning physicist, Richard Feynman, about how meaning can transform work. Initially, physicists at Los Alamos supervised technicians who were ordered to do energy calculations without being told the nature of the project. But "after the task had been imbued with meaning," when J. Robert Oppenheimer explained how important it was to build the bomb before the enemy did, the group worked nearly ten times as fast: "The men were completely transformed. They found new, better ways of doing the work. They invented new programs...they worked through the night." Warren Bennis restates his friend

Charles Handy: "We are all hungry spirits craving purpose and meaning at work, to contribute to something beyond ourselves."

When we asked Dr. Bennis to share a concrete story—a high-point moment in bringing out the best in people, we sensed a man who has continuously chosen to engage fully in life. He spoke about his current experience co-teaching an undergraduate course in the Art and Adventure of Leadership with the president of the University of Southern California, Stephen P. Sample. Bennis is excited about the opportunities they are providing for students to explore who they are and to give them a unique opportunity to be reflective. The students read 1000 pages of text; write eight papers, each of which Bennis reads and comments on; and individually lunch with Bennis for a coaching session on their writing and leadership skills. He stressed the importance of their community outreach, so that students "get exposed to a whole pantheon of role models." He spoke about the "eternal search for our own voice," and rhetorically raised the question as to how leaders bring that out in people: "People don't know what their dreams are."

When questioned about the role of positive affect, such as hope, inspiration, joy, and camaraderie in leading and sustaining change in organizations, Dr. Bennis spoke about how attractive those feelings are, how one wants to be around them, in contrast to "bummer" energy. In his writing, Bennis makes several references to Martin Luther King, Jr., and his efforts to realize his dream. In an *Organization Dynamics* article, "The End of Leadership," he cites Gary Wills, "'[King] tried to lift up others and found himself lifted up in the process....He literally talked himself into useful kinds of trouble. King's oratory urged others on to heroic tasks, and where they went he had to follow.'" Dr. Bennis also commented on the inspiration of Ronald Reagan who, in a time of malaise in the United States, was able to lift up the country with the articulation of hope and inspiration. "Leadership raises the passion quotient, the intensity of attention which mobilizes, animates, and motivates people in constructive activity."

Warren Bennis spoke about both hardiness and "heartiness" which, he reminded us, has shared etymological roots with courage. In commenting on how positive image leads to positive action, he spoke about creating a sense of belonging, hope, and optimism about change by sharing that there is going to be a tomorrow, and by reminding people that they can do things beyond themselves. Dr. Bennis referenced Nelson Mandela's amazing life, his rearing in a particularly challenging culture, his 27 years in jail, and his emergence with awe-inspiring strength—hardiness and heartiness—to lead the people of South Africa.

At the same time, Warren Bennis raised the question as to how extensively we can be socially engineered, given what we know about the "deeply ingrained stuff." Recognizing the genetic complexities, he concludes that there are many ingredients that go into each of us: "We are really a cocktail." Beyond genetics, he also commented on the cultural legacies that exist globally; for example, he said that Belgium, with its history, likely manifests much less optimism than the United States. We need to recognize systemic complexity at individual, group, and societal levels when helping people and their organizations develop beyond their best values.

In speaking about the defining moments in his personal leadership journey, Bennis shared an experience about being in a coffee bar in Massachusetts in the 1960s, when he encountered a man who had just finished several years of psychoanalysis. When he asked him what he had learned, the man responded, "I didn't learn anything, but my friends sure got better." To this point, early in Bennis's career, he saw the power within systems; in this instance, the leverage that occurs when one changes—the system changes.

Warren Bennis also spoke about another defining opportunity that he had been presented with in the military during World War II. In 1944, he was commissioned as a second lieutenant, sent to the European Theater of Operations first as a platoon commander and later as a company commander. At age 19, he was the youngest infantry officer when he led troops in the European theatre. As he writes in *An Invented Life*, "My army experience affirmed my lifelong interest in leadership. The army was the first organization I was able to observe close up and in depth." He illustrates one lesson through discussing a role model, Captain Bessinger, who "really listened to the men, inspired them, and protected them from the whims of the brass." Bessinger embodied what pioneer organization and leadership theorist Douglas McGregor called Theory Y—which is based on the assumption that people are self-motivated.

Douglas McGregor profoundly influenced Warren Bennis in his relentless spirit of inquiry and his career decisions to both teach and provide leadership at universities. It would appear that Bennis has contributed to the establishment of leadership as a field of study, much as McGregor catalyzed the development of organizational studies as a discipline. After his college presidency, McGregor returned to MIT and attracted many extraordinary people, including Bob Greenleaf from AT&T; David Berlew, a Harvard-based psychologist; Harry Levinson, a psychoanalytically trained psychologist from the Menninger Clinic; Don Marquis, president of the American Psychological Association; and Dick Beckhard and Ed Schein, who carried forward McGregor's legacy at the Sloan School and continued to inspire students at MIT for many years. This "accidental group," which included Warren Bennis, had its origins in McGregor's ability to create a generative context. Bennis observed that MIT, with its enviable position as a scientific and technological institute, gave legitimacy to organizational studies that allowed an institutionalization of this discipline. He characterized the contribution as a diaspora, in that the ideas originating at MIT 30 to 40 years ago have been dispersed throughout the United States and the world. In a similar way, Bennis, perhaps more than anyone, has legitimized the study of leadership.

In exploring appreciative relationships, Warren Bennis spoke about the capacity to subordinate one's own ego to the talents of others, commenting that it takes great maturity and esteem to be able to say, "I can't do that." An important question is how to become enough of a self-knower to be appreciative, since "envy eats at the soul." Bennis commented on our strong heritage of competition and winning, and that "testosterone is not limited to just one gender." This provides each of us with issues to work on for a lifetime. He commented that leadership is about character—who we are. The process of becoming a leader is much the same as becoming a fully integrated human being and, in his words, "Life itself is the career." He writes, "To be authentic is literally to be your own author…to discover your own native energies and desires, and then to find your own way of acting on them.…When you write your own life, you have played the game that was natural for you to play."

In extrapolating to a contemporary authored life, Bennis used the example of Alberta Lee, daughter of Wen Ho Lee, a Los Alamos researcher who was recently alleged "the most dangerous spy in the U.S." and unjustly imprisoned for nine months for possible espionage. Alberta, 26, the youngest member of the family and self-acknowledged "brat," mobilized a fundraising and awareness campaign for her father's defense and for Asian Americans as a whole. In a *New York Times* article, this fearless champion acknowledges, "'Now I have a voice. I have a purpose. This is not just for my father. I am speaking for all Asian Americans.'"

Self-knowledge, but not for its own sake, was a recurring theme of our conversation: "Know what your strengths are, which involves a great deal of searching for who you are. But self-knowledge is not necessarily correlated with understanding others: being aware and observant of others is different from self-understanding." Bennis spoke about humility, about taking great effort to listen and observe, which can disconfirm your point of view. "Leaders are deep listeners; they need to understand others and be empathic." Indeed, he seemed quite puzzled with the question as to why we do not more often show our appreciation and acknowledge others. He spoke about how, in contrast, we can be "demeaning," literally taking away meaning from people's lives, whereas through appreciation we free people to flourish.

Our conversation with Warren Bennis ended with the question that he regards as fundamental: How do we develop as human beings? It is the human quest for meaning. In terms of his legacy, Dr. Bennis will undoubtedly be remembered for the wisdom captured in his prolific leadership writings; for his counsel to several U.S. presidents, world and business leaders; and for his contribution to our understanding about group dynamics and social change. Yet he most wants to be remembered by how he touched people's lives in a personal way. He would like to be remembered as a generous person. In our day with him, Warren Bennis demonstrated to each of us how he continues to live his purpose, contributing to our becoming better versions of ourselves.

Chapter Six

The Method, The Model, and Making Meaning

Deanna Riley - Bea Mah Holland - Marjorie Schiller

Method and Model Development

In the fall of 2000, the editors invited 110 professionals and practitioners experienced in Appreciative Inquiry to interview someone they considered an appreciative leader. We were interested in expanding our knowledge of the **competencies** and **attributes** of appreciative leaders, and we especially wanted to understand what differentiates appreciative leaders' thoughts, feelings, and actions.

Competencies have been defined in organizational literature as underlying characteristics of a person that distinguish outstanding performance in a particular job. Competencies can be exhibited in the form of skills, knowledge, social role, self-image, traits or motives. *Webster's Dictionary* defines "**attribute**" as "a quality or characteristic belonging to a person or thing; a distinctive feature."

We intentionally did not provide our authors/interviewers with standards or criteria for defining and selecting appreciative leaders. The intent was to identify characteristics of appreciative leaders by examining the findings from the interviewers. For consistency, a protocol was provided to guide the interviews, and the interviewers were encouraged to add questions that would ensure thorough and unique conversations. Our protocol questions (see Appendix) were intended to elicit information about Appreciative Leadership based on the supposition that these leaders might be strongly relational and participative, rather than commanding and controlling in style and beliefs.

To describe our writers' appreciative leader selection criteria, we initially focused on their examples and stories. The interview responses were read to find traits and characteristics that were common to the 28 leaders who were ultimately interviewed. The traits and characteristics that surfaced became the basis for our identification of fourteen attributes and competencies in our Model

157

of Appreciative Leadership (see Figure A). Like anthropologists, our intent was to be open to patterns in the findings. We recognize that the study of Appreciative Leadership is still in its infancy and the knowledge of appreciative leaders is emergent.

We began to see patterns in the findings. The leadership characteristics seemed to fall naturally into three major clusters: **World View, Practices,** and **Values**. The competencies *envision, inspire,* and *holistic* emerged as what we called **World View**, the conceptual frame and operating philosophy of leaders. We called the next cluster of attributes **Practices** because they explicitly describe the day-to-day behaviors that show what leaders actually do: *challenge, encourage, enable, coach, inquire,* and *dialogue.* The third cluster was labeled **Values** because we recognized the depth of feelings embedded in the stories that the leaders told. The attributes were *genuine, credible,* and *respectful*, and describe the leaders' values and beliefs. Two additional attributes seemed to be bridges between the clusters. *Catalyst* seemed to straddle operating philosophy and day-to-day behaviors and therefore belongs in both the **World View** and **Practices** clusters. Similarly the *relational* attribute is appropriate to both **Practices** and **Values** because it is both belief-based and evident in what people do.

Having derived a tentative model of Appreciative Leadership from the eye of the beholder based on the interviews, we designed a questionnaire to gather demographic data and further information from the writers about what criteria they had actually considered in choosing the leaders they interviewed. We sent a survey (see Appendix) to 30 contributors. Twenty-eight responded.

We learned that the majority of the leaders (25) were from various regions in North America and that there was also an international flavor with leaders from Europe, Mexico, and New Zealand. Private industry had the greatest representation with 16 leaders, followed by eight in education, and four in government. Fifteen of those interviewed worked in not-for-profit organizations and 13 in the for-profit sector. There were 16 men and 12 women; 21 Caucasians, four African-Americans, two Asians, and one Hispanic. Their ages fell into a bell curve with forty- and fifty-year-olds in the center. There were thirty-year-olds on one end and

Model of
Appreciative Leadership

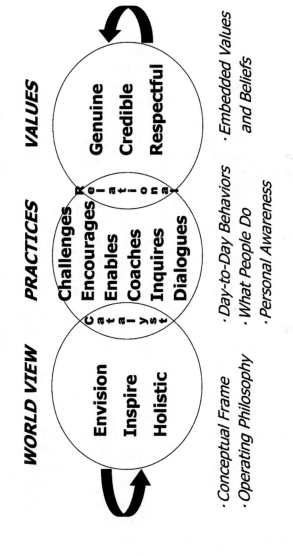

WORLD VIEW   **PRACTICES**   **VALUES**

Envision
Inspire
Holistic

Catalyst

Challenges
Encourages
Enables
Coaches
Inquires
Dialogues

Relational

Genuine
Credible
Respectful

· Conceptual Frame
· Operating Philosophy

· Day-to-Day Behaviors
· What People Do
· Personal Awareness

· Embedded Values
  and Beliefs

(FIGURE A)   Source Deanna Riley

people of sixty and older on the other. There were no "twenty-somethings," but leaders in their seventies are represented (see Chapter 5, "Reflections of a Lifetime").

In the survey, writers were asked to rate the "importance as an attribute/competency for selection" of the fourteen elements we had identified. This was intended to gain further insight into which competencies were important to these writers in selecting their leaders and to further validate the Model of Appreciative Leadership. The writers were also invited to add comments. There were some differences in what the writers said guided their choice of a leader. For instance, some contributors who interviewed in large for-profit settings mentioned considerations that concentrated on organizational impact, such as the ability to drive long-term change, affect corporate climate, be a power broker, and initiate a significant culture shift. Some of the more seasoned and experienced contributors paid greater attention to strategic and whole-systems thinking. The experience of the interviewer seemed to influence the degree of expected complexity.

The attributes and competencies that our contributors ranked highest in importance in their considerations—from the field of fourteen—were the abilities to be *genuine, credible,* and *respectful.* There was a remarkable consistency. In fact, all the authors selected as their first, second, and third choices, the competencies that we had placed in the **Values** cluster, although they were not labeled as such in the survey. The competencies and attributes in the cluster we called **World View**, *envision, inspire,* and *holistic,* as well as the bridge attribute *catalyst,* were the next highest ranked group by our interviewers. The competencies in our **Practices** cluster, *challenges, encourages, enables, coaches, inquires,* and *dialogues,* and the bridge attribute *relational,* were ranked third. In the Model of Appreciative Leadership, appreciative leaders translate their **World View**, their basic views and intentions, into effective **Practices.** These behaviors show how appreciative leaders connect with others. **Values** are the lens we use to see and evaluate those day-to-day behaviors or **Practices.** These are the checks and balances that show leaders act on what they value, the hallmark of appreciative leaders.

160

Chris Argyris, a well-known management educator, has written extensively about the gap that often occurs between what he calls "espoused theory" and "theory in practice." According to our interviewers, these leaders have closed that gap. We believe the attributes of the **Values** cluster are the essence of authenticity and credibility. What the writers said, loud and clear, is that what differentiated these leaders as appreciative leaders is that they "live their values out loud." These men and women are intrinsically values based. It is the continuous core that drives their actions and decisions. They operate on a day-to-day basis from intensely held values. For all of the leaders you have read about in this book, everything begins and ends with values.

Based on qualitative analysis of survey ratings and comments, we gained insight into the thoughts, feelings, and actions of appreciative leaders. They uniformly exhibit a seemingly unconditional positive attitude; they have a positive nature and appear to be hopeful and optimistic. They express openness to growth, ideas, diversity, and situations and conditions that challenge traditional, established ways. They express moderation and fairness, and they seek to understand. These leaders are very open about their spirituality; they speak about the roots of their beliefs and link those beliefs to their philosophy of leading and everyday behavior. They seem to understand their own and others' need for meaning and significance in their work and daily lives.

Linking Theory and Practice

The competencies and attributes that the writers saw in these appreciative leaders resonates with those described in twentieth-century organizational behavior classics such as Robert Greenleaf's *Servant Leadership*, Peter Block's *Stewardship*, James Collins and Jerry Porras's *Built to Last*, Stephen Covey's *Principle Centered Leadership,* James Kouzes and Barry Posner's *Leadership,* Abraham Maslow's *Motivation and Personality*, Douglas McGregor's *The Human Side of Enterprise*, Peter Drucker's *Managing for the Future*, James McGregor Burns's *Leadership*, and Warren Bennis's prolific writings.

The following findings reflect the insights and learnings from 28 interviews, 15 of which are included in this book. To get the full picture and expand your knowledge of appreciative leaders, we suggest that you read additional interviews on the Taos Institute website at <www.taosinstitute.org>, and in the special November 2001 Appreciative Leadership issue of the *International Appreciative Inquiry Newsletter* at <www.aradford.co.uk>.

The themes that emerged from integrating interview and survey information capture the characteristics of appreciative leaders— and correlate to the attributes and competencies in the **World View**, **Practices**, and **Values** clusters in the Model.

- Appreciative leaders are belief-based, with an explicit spiritual orientation and practice.
- Leadership lives in the group and not in any one person.
- Multiple truths exist in ways of thinking, doing, and being.
- Appreciative leaders have an unwavering commitment to bringing out the best in themselves and others.
- Appreciative leaders find generative forces in their many circumstances and multiple systems.

Examples from the interviews that exemplify these themes follow.

Theme 1. Leaders Are Belief-based with an Explicit Spiritual Orientation and Practice

*Consistent with the attributes of the **Values** cluster in the Model of Appreciative Leadership—genuine, credible, and respectful— the leaders demonstrate their optimistic and realistic views of the people with whom they work. Because of their trust in, and the openness of, their beliefs and values, they create a reinforcing cycle of affirmation.*

Virtually all of the leaders interviewed spoke about their belief in their fellow human beings. Several noted that, as young workers, mentors had demonstrated faith in them beyond the faith that they had in themselves. These appreciative leaders are now replicating that behavior in working with their associates.

Ricky Lewis, an African American manager at Verizon, spoke about making mistakes in his career, and realized that a mentor who had unwavering faith in him not only guided him but also took on an oppositional force to champion his success. Lewis is now "passing it on."

Lee Olivier of Millstone Nuclear Power Plant recalled his mentor as a man who "blew on the ember," and had an intuitive appreciation for what he [Lee] could do. He helped Lee realize, "You can get people to follow you." In a similar vein, Kenny Lang of BP reported about a mentor: "I've tried to make what Andrew gave me available to all of my reports in terms of creating time [for them], as often as they need."

We were surprised to hear that the majority of appreciative leaders spoke openly about their personal spirituality. Their spirituality base took many forms, including mysticism, Christianity, and personal meaning systems.

At Green Mountain Coffee, CEO Bob Stiller's "commitment to his company's social mission and to the people who work for him and with him is deeply rooted in his personal values and spiritual beliefs." As a seventeen-year employee of the company noted, "Bob truly believes we are working for a higher cause, and he imparts that to all of us."

For Kenny Lang, VP at British Petroleum, one of the most important events in his life was his religious conversion. His faith shows up in the way he frames his work. In speaking about a merger with his organization, he aspires to the time when "two are cooperating effectively, when each sees and elicits and works towards the best of what the other brings."

Theme 2. Leadership Lives in the Group and Not in Any One Person

Team leadership is a predominant and recurring theme. There is a belief that leadership capabilities reside in the group and not in the designated leader alone. There is an explicit acknowledgment that individuals alone do not have the answers. At the same time, people are viewed as having the capacity to do what needs to be done. In the Model of Appreciative Leadership, this relates to the competencies and attributes of envision, inspire, and holistic in the **World View** *cluster and the bridging competency of catalyst between* **World View** *and* **Practices.** *For appreciative leaders a critical*

163

*imperative for organizational success today is "the collective discovery of the way forward," with the realization that this **World View** is not only about being inclusive, it is also good business.*

The Civil Rights efforts and other social movements illustrate passion and motivation sustained by principles, and not just by individuals. "Doc" Lafayette is one of countless leaders who lived out principles within the Civil Rights movement in order to elevate society's norms of equality and justice.

Annette Griffin, a superintendent of schools, tells the story of a demoralized school district that she inherited: "I needed to help people realize that there were better days ahead and we are all in this together." She created conditions so that people experienced ownership and felt a part of the organization. By the end of her tenure as a superintendent, the staff had recaptured their esteem and developed ways to sustain the new strengthened culture. They had internalized the necessary change.

Another appreciative leader, Bob Stiller, CEO of Green Mountain Coffee, said, "The organization's intention—the culture—is what happens when no one is around. The culture must fully leverage people." To fulfill this intention, Stiller ensures "a clear, shared goal, sense of purpose, sense of trust in the whole, and a full engagement of people with the support they need to act."

Appreciative leaders manifested humility in the acknowledgment of their "not knowing." Said Thomas Inui, president of the Fetzer Institute, "In the crucible of the toughest stuff they do, there is nothing to trust except community and collaboration within it."

Theme 3. Multiple Truths Exist in Ways of Thinking, Doing, and Being

Traditionally, leaders have often been expected to be heroic and find the "one right way" to proceed. However, these appreciative leaders saw that there were many ways to deal with situations; often, there were multiple paths and many truths. Yet there was one consistency: these leaders played the role of architect, designing the structure in which a process could enable the development of an empowered community of people. From this

World View, they held the space that allowed the emergence of people's creative abilities. As David Cooperrider notes in his Foreword to this volume, "...humility is a stronger quality of leadership than bravado, infectious curiosity more important than supervision...."

Warren Bennis, who speaks from a lifetime as a leader and writer said, "It takes great maturity and esteem to say, 'I can't do that.'" This is illustrated by Tom Inui of the Fetzer Institute, who recalled that he learned how to deal with anxiety by admitting ignorance. He showed others that it was all right to lack knowledge. This led to learning with other people rather than lecturing and, more important, it modeled for others that it was acceptable to "not know."

Similarly, Police Chief Peter Carnes of Yarmouth, Massachusetts, obtained citizen input about building the police headquarters on town-owned land. Because of a conversation between a concerned citizen and the approachable police chief, the town saved substantial money. Carnes's reputation as a community builder demonstrates the power of one person to dramatically change the community ethos. Because he hears and values citizens, he has been integral in developing a strong community.

In another example of discovering alternatives, frequently mandated overtime at Hunter Douglas was a problem. Working with the business units, groups of people came up with customized solutions, including streamlining work, flexible schedules, and work-at-home options. Rick Pellett and Mike Burns, two appreciative leaders, said, "We encourage them to think and act differently—to question the status quo."

Theme 4. Appreciative Leaders Have an Unwavering Commitment to Bringing out the Best in Themselves and Others

*These leaders led through appreciation, encouragement, validation, and support of people's best talents, and provided the structure for appreciative dialogue. Their behaviors reflect the attributes and competencies that were clustered under **Practices** in the Model—* challenge, encourage, enable, coach, inquire, *and* dialogue.

Sarah Eagger, a physician from England, sets aside informal space and time for creating the conditions for building relationships. "Appreciative relationships in this team are also about being with each other—taking some time to know each other as people, knowing what is going on in each others' lives, and having some social time to get together." On the other hand, Lee Olivier of the Millstone Nuclear Power Plant held more formal "In Touch" sessions with employees, where he listened and responded to spontaneous questions, concerns, and suggestions.

Mike Green, the CEO of Concord Hospital, is credited with welcoming input from others. As he said, "I try to be just Mike. If you see my door is open, come in. At hospital town meetings, everyone is encouraged to come, provide feedback, and ask questions."

Kathi Mullin, a program director in the Boston Public Schools, is described by a colleague as having created "an ethos of caring and commitment." Kathi herself reported, "I am a person of strong conviction. I truly believe that if you can build environments where young people are really engaged, motivated to learn, and have caring adults in their lives, you can make a difference. That's what I'm about."

Other themes that emerged here were "allowing people to make mistakes" and challenging them beyond their own perceived capabilities.

At Hunter Douglas, Mike Burns spoke about supporting people to do what they love and do best: "Give people chances to experiment and make sure they succeed." Rick Pellett advises, "Don't try to fix yourself or other people. Just figure out a way to work around people's weaknesses and play to their strengths."

Retired educator Dolph Norton is repeatedly saluted by many of his protégés who speak about the investment of time he makes in people. They credit much of their professional success to his counsel. One young woman for whom Dolph was a mentor told the story of how he patiently listened to her describe one of her key challenges, and, to her amazement, he helped her "conceptualize the confusing issues in seconds."

Theme 5. Appreciative Leaders Find Generative Forces in Their Many Circumstances and Multiple Systems

*The appreciative leaders used generative language and engaged in conversations that often led to new and creative approaches to problem solving or inspiring new ventures. They spoke of the criticality of questioning and listening. They were able to think "out of the box, in very diverse contexts." Operating in fluid work environments, these leaders listened to others—not only to their direct reports, but also to people in the whole organization and beyond—and developed methods and mindsets that seemed to accelerate learning and the diffusion of positive understanding and action. Several of the leaders were noted for their holistic conceptual frame that enabled them to see the interconnections among the individuals, the team, the organization, and the organization's place in the world. Leaders stood up for non-traditional positions, which catalyzed their culture to shift dramatically. These behaviors and operating philosophies resonate with the competencies and attributes of **World View** and **Practices**.*

Margaret Crawford of Harley-Davidson is enriched through listening, particularly listening to those who hold points of view different from her own. She suggests: "Seek out people with different perspectives. It's the people with different perspectives that you learn the most from. Ask yourself, what can I learn from this person? Learn through their experience."

And when Mike Burns from Hunter Douglas was asked what he wishes he would have known earlier on, he responded, "Listen, listen, listen! At first I always had the answers and told people what they had to do. It took me years to understand that listening to people is your key to success—and your key to *their* success."

Dave Cooperrider has often said that inquiry is the most important word in the field of Appreciative Inquiry. All of the Leaders who were interviewed in the Appreciative Leaders Project said something about learning, listening, reading, teaching, or participating in training programs and their own personal growth. This is a curious collection of people who thrive on the renewal and refreshment of continual learning and personal growth through many means, including feedback, meditation, reading, reflection, coaching, courses and prayer..

"In all of his interactions, Lee [Olivier] fostered a climate of inquiry...[Lee] doesn't wait for mentoring and encouragement to show up. His spirit of inquiry...is obvious as he searches far and wide for answers, learning from experts he will never meet in person."

School Superintendent Annette Griffin believes, "Telling doesn't work. I invite people to question—to dialogue—to discover ways we've never tried before, so that all children have a chance for success. We use inquiry in almost every interaction in management meetings."

In Conclusion

The appreciative leaders are strongly values-driven. This is not the application of technique or "fake it until you make it." This is an authentic congruence of belief and action. The interviewers, seasoned practitioners, perceived these leaders as credible people who walked their talk and were inclusive in their actions beyond the rhetoric. There was agreement among the writers that you can't simulate it; either you are "the genuine article" or you're not. The leaders were seen as, and served as, role models in their organizations. They were regarded as particularly open people who naturally created a safe community. These leaders recognize the power of the positive, seek answers from what has worked, live their spirituality, and develop the best in people. Their stories indicate the effectiveness of and provide a direction for an appreciative approach to leadership in today's organizations. The model developed from our survey is a beginning, indicating a path for the future. We hope it will provide a template for future appreciative leaders.

Appendix

This appendix contains the following reference materials:

- Interview Protocol

- Interviewer Survey

- Interviewer Biographies

- Related Resources

Interview Protocol

Appreciative Leaders:
In the Eye of The Beholder

"We are what we think....With our thoughts we make our world."
Gautama Buddha

TOPIC 1: The Task of Bringing out the Best in Human Beings and Organizations

Peter Drucker said that management is about joint performance. He said, "Leadership is about creating an ALIGNMENT OF STRENGTHS and making people's weaknesses irrelevant."

a. Please share with me: What have you learned, in practical ways, about bringing out the best in human beings, groups, and organizations as a whole? How do you bring out the best?

b. Now, can you share a concrete story—a "high-point" moment in bringing out the best in people?

c. Who do you remember really appreciating you? How were you aware of their appreciation? What did they do?

TOPIC 2: Appreciative Relationships

a. As you think about the role of appreciation in close working relationships, how have you developed feedback-rich environments?

b. What in your experience produces working relationships that are authentic, appreciative, and accepting?

Mergers and acquisitions call for the highest levels of collaboration and cooperation as expressed in the Hindu greeting of *namaste*. *Namaste* means, "May the God in you meet the God in me and together we are one."

c.   How do we both protect and expand in that context? What advice can you give to those who are collaborating, cooperating, and merging?

TOPIC 3: Positive Image and Positive Action

Aristotle once said, "A vivid imagination compels the whole body to obey it," and Einstein once said, "Imagination is more important than knowledge."

a.   Where and how in organizational life do new, dynamic, and compelling positive images of the future come from?

b.   How do you help people and organizations go beyond even their most positive visions and develop beyond their best values?

A great deal of time and money has been spent studying pathology. For the first time the American Psychological Association is putting funds into studying healthy minds.

c.   What is the importance, the significance of positive thinking in your life— as a human being, a leader, a parent, a partner, etc.? What images do you hold?

TOPIC 4: The Spirit of Inquiry

Would you put the spotlight on inquiry? Please flesh out and speak about the spirit of inquiry.

a. How does inquiry live in you as a leader and in the organizations you have led?

b. Ken Blanchard talks about catching people doing something right. How do we replicate, disseminate, and internalize the learnings from our successes?

TOPIC 5:The Role of Positive Affect in Bringing Out the Best

Bureaucratic theory has seriously underestimated the role of positive affect—things like hope, inspiration, joy, camaraderie—in leading and sustaining change in organizations. At the same time, recent medical science has demonstrated the role of positive affect in being healthy.

a. I'd like to explore your experience and your thoughts about the role of hope, or inspiration, or joy, or confidence, or camaraderie—in bringing out the best in human systems. Which of these words has a story in your life as a leader?

b. What have been the defining moments or choice points in your own leadership journey?

c. How has your leadership philosophy shaped the choices that you have made?

a. As you look back on your leadership career what advice do you wish you had been given, what would have saved you bumping into walls, and what would you tell others about being a leader?

Appreciative Leader Interviews:
Survey of Contributors
5/1/01

(please complete)
> **Interviewer:**
> **Leader:**

1. Please provide the following demographic information so we can identify any similarities or differences among the leaders who were interviewed.
The *appreciative leader* you chose was:
    a. Business Culture (Please underline one)
        > American/Canadian
        > European
        > Asian
        > Mexico/Central/South America
        > Other_____
    b. Sector (Please underline one)
        > Government   Education   Private Industry
        > Voluntary Organization
    c. Category (Please underline one)
        > For Profit   Not-For-Profit
    d. Demographics (Please complete)
        > • Gender -
        > • Ethnicity/Race -
        > • Other -
        > (Age/Region/Communities of Commonality)

2. **In order to understand the nature of Appreciative Leadership, we want to know what criteria you used to select the appreciative leader you interviewed. We have extracted a list of attributes/ competencies from all of the interviews and have listed them in the following table. Based on your impression of the person you selected,** *please rate each item below by <u>underlining</u> the number which most closely characterizes your appreciative leader.* **Rate each item** *first on its importance* **in how you selected your leader; and** *second on the skill level/ability* **your leader possesses for each item. The rating scale is shown above each column.**

175

	Importance	Skill level/Ability
	1=Not at all important	1=Nottat all skilled/able
	2	2
	3	3
	4	4
	5=Critically important	5=Highly skilled/able

Attributes/Competencies	Importance as an attribute/ competency for selection					Skill level/Ability of your leader in this attribute or competency				
Envision - creates positive images of desired futures with understanding of current reality and organization history.	1	2	3	4	5	1	2	3	4	5
Inspire - tests the status quo; takes a position and accepts accountability for that position; stands up for beliefs.	1	2	3	4	5	1	2	3	4	5
Holistic - recognizes critical interconnections within the system and ensures they are integrated to create value.	1	2	3	4	5	1	2	3	4	5
Catalyst - focuses and energizes a group to accomplish change together.	1	2	3	4	5	1	2	3	4	5
Challenges - believes in people and holds them accountable.	1	2	3	4	5	1	2	3	4	5
Encourages - Highlights accomplishments and progress. Advocates for people.	1	2	3	4	5	1	2	3	4	5
Enables - influences through specific encouragement, support and positive feedback.	1	2	3	4	5	1	2	3	4	5
Coaches - builds capability through thoughtful affirmation and development of people's strengths.	1	2	3	4	5	1	2	3	4	5
Inquires - intense desire to know more—questions; engages in learning and co-creation with others.	1	2	3	4	5	1	2	3	4	5
Dialogues - persuasively presents and articulates; actively listens; is open to feedback.	1	2	3	4	5	1	2	3	4	5
Relational - derives intrinsic satisfaction from relationship—deep desire to work with others.	1	2	3	4	5	1	2	3	4	5
Genuine - "walks the talk"—acts in accordance with expressed beliefs and values.	1	2	3	4	5	1	2	3	4	5
Credible - instills trust through personal openness and honesty.	1	2	3	4	5	1	2	3	4	5
Respectful - optimistic and realistic view of individuals and groups; inclusive; honors differences of opinion and ideas.	1	2	3	4	5	1	2	3	4	5

2. Were there other attributes/competencies that influenced your choice of an appreciative leader? If so, please list and define them below and rate their importance to your selection and the skill level/ability of your leader as you did in question 2.

Importance	Skill level/Ability
1=Not at all important	1=Not at all skilled/able
2	2
3	3
4	4
5=Critically important	5=Highly skilled/able

Attributes/Competencies	Importance as an attribute/ competency for selection					Skill level/Ability of your leader in this attribute or competency				
	1	2	3	4	5	1	2	3	4	5
	1	2	3	4	5	1	2	3	4	5
	1	2	3	4	5	1	2	3	4	5
	1	2	3	4	5	1	2	3	4	5
	1	2	3	4	5	1	2	3	4	5

3. Is there anything else we should know that influenced your choice of this leader?

4. Do you have any other thoughts or comments?

177

Interviewer Biographies

Kristine Crowell attended the University of Wisconsin, Whitewater, graduating with a Business Administration degree. She is currently a member of the Air National Guard as an Executive Officer. Kristine earned her Master's in Business Administration from the University of Wisconsin, Parkside, and is employed by Harley-Davidson as an Organizational Excellence Program Manager.

Jeff Doyle is the Assistant Vice President for Student Affairs at Shenandoah University. Jeff has a PhD in Higher Education from the University of Virginia with a minor in Leadership from Darden Business School. Jeff has served in a variety of higher education areas and has BA and MEd degrees from the University of Virginia.

Christopher Flaugh, part of Verizon Corporate Real Estate's Quality and Performance Assurance group, has been with the company since 1998. He was formerly an independent consultant, and also has product management and start-up experience with several U.S. lotteries. He resides in Dallas, Texas, with his dog, Maxine.

Gerry Gallagher completed a 41-year career with FMC Corporation as a research chemist, salesman, and manager in research, sales, and marketing. Now on Cape Cod, he is a court mediator, elder care ombudsman, and organizational consultant. He studied Appreciative Inquiry at Benedictine University with Mary Ann Rainey and Peter Sorenson.

Bea Mah Holland is a consultant, coach, teacher, and writer. Formerly president of Pegasus Communications, she has held a variety of other roles in business, education, healthcare, and government, including Leadership Program Manager at Digital Equipment Corporation, Director of Leadership at the MIT Sloan School of Management, and editor at the Harvard Educational Review. *Her doctorate from Harvard University concentrated on organizational effectiveness and adult learning.*

Gene Knott is a Diplomate in Counseling Psychology and faculty member in Human Development and Family Studies at the University of Rhode Island. He has also been a psychotherapist, executive coach, management consultant, and frequent presenter in a 30-year practice in human services, high technology, health care, and higher education internationally.

Bernard J. Mohr *is president of The Synapse Group, Inc., an international consultancy specializing in the leadership, planning, and execution of strategic change involving people, technology, culture, and business processes. He is coauthor of* Appreciative Inquiry: Change at the Speed of Imagination *(2001), and developed North America's first advanced workshop and first Field Practicum in Appreciative Inquiry.*

Joan Murray *has worked in Organizational Development at Concord Hospital for 16 years, helping people enhance interpersonal and team skills, leadership, and customer service. Joan is a graduate of Albany College of Pharmacy in New York and New Hampshire College Graduate School. She enjoys learning and skiing.*

Nancy Oelklaus's *passion is releasing human potential. Her articles have appeared in* The American School Board Journal *and* The Systems Thinker. *A native of Oklahoma, Oelklaus has two grown children and two granddaughters, Madeline and Mallari. A graduate of Texas A&M University at Commerce, Oelklaus coaches school leaders and facilitates educational change. She serves on the board of Visions of a Better World Foundation.*

Judy Otto *has worked in leadership, organizational, and team development in both the private and public sector for 25 years, helping organizations, work units, and individuals plan, implement, and manage change. She is also an adjunct faculty member of The Center for Creative Leadership and the Rensselaer Learning Institute.*

Anne Radford *is an organizational consultant working with businesses, government, and community groups in Europe. From her base in London she coaches managers and consultants in their use of Appreciative Inquiry and edits the AI quarterly e-mail newsletter. Anne is a founding member of the Appreciative Inquiry Consulting Group (AIC).*

Amanda Trosten-Bloom *is a Director of Consulting Services with the Corporation for Positive Change. One of the first consultants to use Appreciative Inquiry for whole-system culture change, she now teaches and consults on AI-based positive change. Together with Diana Whitney, she is co-author of* Positive Change Works! *(publication pending).*

Joan Vitello *is an internationally known leader, editor, author, consultant, and speaker. Joan is a past president of the American Association of Critical Care Nurses and is currently an associate with the Institute for Nursing Healthcare Institute, Boston, Massachusetts. She received a PhD in Human and Organizational Systems from the Fielding Institute in July 2001 after completing her dissertation on emotional intelligence.*

Ilene Wasserman, principal of Innovative Communities at the Workplace (ICW Consulting Group), has been in practice as an organizational development consultant for 20 years. She was the lead consultant for the Green Mountain Coffee Roasters Appreciative Inquiry initiative. She is a founding member of the Broccoli Alliance, a member of the Appreciative Inquiry Consortium, and has presented case studies of her work at professional conferences.

Penny Williamson is Associate Professor of Medicine, Johns Hopkins University School of Medicine, and an independent consultant. She teaches physicians communication, teaching, and leadership skills and leads renewal retreats for professionals from myriad fields. Penny helps leadership groups and organizations build sustainable capacities in relationship-centered work and collaborative decision-making.

Linda Winner, Director, Center for Executive Leadership, and Senior Faculty member at the Federal Executive Institute, previously served as Director of Alumni Continuing Education at the University of North Carolina (UNC)-Chapel Hill, Assistant Professor and Director of Leadership Development at the University of Virginia's Center for Public Service, and Director of Continuing Education at UNC-Asheville. Linda has BA, MA and PhD degrees from UNC-Chapel Hill.

Related Resources

The following list, although not all inclusive, is a good starting point for readers who would like to know more about the principles and practices underlying Appreciative Leadership. This material is current. New books and other resources will become available. Please check the electronic references for updates.

Books

Bushe, Gervase R., *Clear Leadership: How Outstanding Leaders Make Themselves Understood, Cut Through the Mush, and Help Everyone Get Real at Work,* Davies-Black, 2001. ISBN 0 89106 152 5

Cooperrider, David and Diana Whitney, *Collaborating for Change: Appreciative Inquiry,* Berrett-Koehler, 2000. ISBN 1 58376 044 X

Elliott, Charles, *Locating the Energy for Change: An Introduction to Appreciative Inquiry*, International Institute for Sustainable Development, 1999. ISBN 1 89553 615 4

Gergen, Kenneth, *An Invitation to Social Construction*, Sage Publications, 1999. ISBN 0 80398 377 8

Srivastva, Suresh and David Cooperrider, *Appreciative Management and Leadership: The Power of Positive Thought and Action in Organizations*, Jossey-Bass, 1990. ISBN 1 55542 236 5

Watkins, Jane Magruder and Bernard J. Mohr, *Appreciative Inquiry, Change at the Speed of Imagination,* Jossey-Bass, 2001. ISBN 0 78795 179 X

Weisbord, Marvin, *Discovering Common Ground,* Berrett-Koehler, 1992. ISBN 1 88105 208 7

Electronic References

Appreciative Inquiry Listserv, *<www.ailist@business.utah.edu>*

Appreciative Inquiry Newsletter, *<www.aradford.co.uk>*

Case Western Reserve University, Weatherhead School of Management, *<www.connection.cwru.edu/ai>*

Taos Institute, *<www.taosinstitute.org>*